It wasn't *a dark and stormy night*, it was an advertisement on the back page of the 'Sunday Supplement' offering a real sailboat for the end off of a carton of KOOL cigarettes and eighty-eight dollars. I was currently smoking KOOL's so it appeared to be seen as a coincidence…. or fate, as you'll see.

The design was designated "Snark"; eight feet long with a beam of three and a half feet and carried a forty-five-square foot sail in a "lateen rig" layout. The hull was made of Styrofoam, in this offering. It looked like it could be fun. I had to have it. So, taking my hard-earned eighty-eight dollars and the other end of my current carton of KOOLs, I was on my way into the 'nautical world'.

KOOL Cigarette's "Snark"

Finally, after anxious days of expectations, "She" arrived via UPS, right to the front door of Peggy's house. Peggy was my next-door neighbor and would be my wife in the very near future. (Ships/boats are referred to in the "female" gender.)

Getting it inside wasn't a problem…the Styrofoam hull was pretty light and the mast and boom were aluminum

1

plus lines (what you call ropes in the nautical world; much more of that to come) and the plywood center-board and rudder. It was all well packaged in a cardboard carton that was more awkward to handle than any weight factor. We managed to muscle it in to the living-room.... opened the carton and laid-out the pieces. There it was, the "Snark" ...a sailboat? It sure didn't look like much of one-- is this thing going to hold two people?

The *"some assembly required"* didn't take long and reading the assembly instructions one learned some nautical terms; --like that stick attached to the rudder is called the "Tiller" ...or that line that raises the sail is called a "Halyard" and the line controlling the sail is called the "Sheet". Many of the nautical terms have slid over into aviation so it wasn't a complete 're-training event' for me. (Early on I had reached my life goal of becoming a pilot.)

The following day Peggy helped me tie Snark to the top of my very black, very long Cadillac and decided to head down to Meydenbauer Bay to launch our Snark. During the drive Peggy was reading some more of the instructions to me.

I asked, "That's all good, but what happens when the wind hits the sail?"

Her answer was, "I'm getting to that, this next section is about *capsizing!*"

After recovering from the laughter that ensued and arriving at Meydenbauer Bay, I found a place to park and unloaded our craft and prepared to put it in the water. Assembly was quickly accomplished and we were ready for our first sail. I told Peggy to get in, not knowing at the time that she was very uncomfortable when being in, or *on*, water that was deep enough to be over her head. (More about that subject later.)

A light breeze was playing across the large bay, just right for our inaugural sail. The Instruction Manual that Peggy had been reading out to me as we drove down, suggested trying the various "points of sail" to experience the effectiveness of sail, center board and rudder.

It was all going well until a 'smart-ass' in a ski boat came by *wa-ay* too close, nearly swamping us. The real small eight-foot hull and barely wide enough beam, felt pretty small when waves over a foot tall were raining down on us. It wasn't quite a 'laundry-issue" on my part but I was concerned about Peggy.

After thinking that we had now *'learned how to sail'* it was time to load up and head home. As I was taking the Snark out of the water I noticed that Peggy had left 'hand-indentations' in the coaming (edge) of the Styrofoam hull. –hmm, I wondered about that.

My Sister, Patsy, lived nearby and we stopped by to pay our respects and to show off our 'yacht'. The Love family had been boaters for some time and welcomed us to the wonderful world of boats.

That being said, I'm turning over the lead in this joint venture of writing about boating in the Northwest.

Patsy?

TWO

PATSY REMEMBERS
Our First Boat, the "NO NAME"

It was 1967. My husband, Hal, drove into the driveway, jumped out of the car and burst into the kitchen exclaiming, "Hi Honey. Jim and I just came back from the Seattle boat Show—the one that is held at the Key Arena at Seattle Center." He went on to say, "The Exposition was mostly focused on commercial boats and fishermen. There were a few boats and booths selling fishing gear."

"What did you buy," I asked. "--a new lure to catch bigger salmon?"

"Well no…. (Hal hesitated) …uh, we bought a boat."

"But Hal, you know we can't afford a boat right now!" This was beginning to sound a bit worrisome.

"Patsy, it only cost a hundred dollars…fifty from me and fifty from Jim. Well, the oars were extra."

Jim Crowder was Hal's best buddy, fishing partner, Best Man at his and Patsy's wedding and probably more.

"C'mon Patsy, I'll show you…it's in the car." He took her hand leading her out the kitchen door to the back driveway.

And there it was, lying on her side in the back of their station wagon. With my lending a hand, we pulled it out of the car. There it was, our first boat. It was blue, molded plastic, about eight feet long but it was a boat.

"Oh good, it's just the right size for Keyport," I remarked. (She was referring to the summer place where Jim's family, the 'Crowders' had a cottage.) "Have you thought of a name?" Patsy asked Hal. He shook his head.

"Well then, how about 'NO NAME'?" It stuck.

This eight-foot plastic boat was not the right one for 'salmon fishing', Jim and Hal's favorite pastime. It wouldn't support a motor to take them to the various salmon fishing grounds known to the two fishermen. However, it was a boat and the beginning of the dreaded 'boat-i-tis' for the Love family.

Jim was the first to succumb to the "i-tis" and purchased a runabout that was equipped with a large 'outboard motor' that would suffice for the time being.

NO NAME did end up at Keyport, where the kids learned to row in the calm Puget Sound waters of Dogfish Bay. Our grandson Dylan remembers.... his grandfather said, "Right after dinner, we will wait until dark to row out to the middle of Dogfish Bay where we can dump the day's garbage. That's when the dogfish will swim over to gobble it up." The garbage draws a bit of a crowd. The dogfish is a small member of the 'shark family', and gets pretty excitedly aggressive with an eating frenzy.

Hal would hold a flashlight towards the water to watch the dogfish attack the meal. One could see their fins slicing through the water coming in force to engage in the feast.

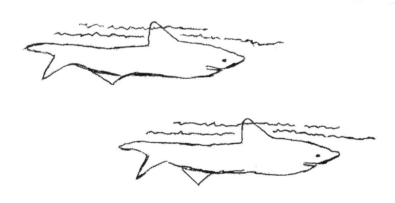

Oh Boy! Food, food food! Um...YUMMY!!

Jim Crowder towing his runabout in "Dogfish Bay, Keyport

That 8-ft. boat sure looks small.

There was an event worth talking about that is actually about Jim's boat. Since we had the room at our home in Bellevue, Jim had stored his boat and trailer in our driveway.

And, for that matter, my brother Michael also stored his SNARK at our house, which was near Meydenbauer Bay.

This is a story that is actually about our family dog, Wolf, and his introduction to boating. His adventure started when Dad decided to try out the boat/trailer that Jim had stored in our driveway. "It runs fine, try it out." Jim had said.

Dad attached the trailer/boat to our car, and at the last minute asked Wolf to come along for the ride. When he reached the boat ramp at Newport Shore he backed the trailer to the water's edge, and rolled the boat off, then parked car and trailer in the adjacent lot.

Hal pushed the boat into the water and jumped in. "Okay Wolf, come on, get in…we can go for a little ride."

Dad pulled the starter-cord, put the engine in gear, reached for the throttle, and the boat took off, full speed ahead out into Lake Washington…. that is until Hal looked down and saw that the boat was filling with water. --he had neglected to put the *Drain Plug* back into the drain hole.

This emergency situation called for quick action. Dad yelled, "Wolf, you are going to steer the boat on a straight course while I find the plug and put it in the drain hole." He placed Wolf's paws between the spokes of the steering wheel and rushed back to find the plug while the boat was planing. (With the boat, up and planing, less water was coming in, than would be the case if they were stopped.) Their combined effort worked. --Man, and his faithful dog once again rising to the need!

They came home with a story to tell after an exciting boat ride.

After hearing the story, I questioned, "Do you really expect me to believe that…I would have to see it."

Hal grabbed a pencil and some paper and set to work, explaining as he sketched. (I'm including the sketch here for you, the reader, to see as well.)

That's it for now.   *…. your turn Michael.*

THREE   A BIGGER BOAT

Our friend Jim England had a house on Yarrow Bay, Lake Washington. He was a member of The Seattle Yacht Club. In fact, it was Jim England that pushed me over the edge into the world of boats. I had always had an interest but it was Jim that asked me if I would like to become a partner on his forty some odd foot Tri-Cabin Chriscraft. I asked, "How can I do that?" ...he said to just pay the moorage and the insurance and we'd work something out from there.

He invited Peggy and me to go on a "Computed Log" race. This is calculating time-distance over a known course and then making it happen. Since this was akin to the world of aviation it was sorta like watching paint dry for me, but a reason to go boating.

The 'course' was from the locks, across the sound to Bremerton and back. Upon returning we pulled over to the gas dock and Jim put over a hundred dollars' worth of gasoline into the tank. I might add, this was when gas was about fifty cents a gallon. I helped pay but told Jim that I couldn't afford hundred-dollar weekends and thought I'd look into the world of sail.

Jim understood and told us that the club was getting rid of their Penguin fleet, replacing them with 'C-Larks'. (Both Penguin and C-Larks were "Racing Class" boats, the latter being larger and more advanced.) The Penguins were being offered to club members at a ridiculous price. I purchased one through Jim and he bought one as well. This gave us two Penguins at his house.

It was a fun summer with lots of lawn parties and sailing. Peggy's two older kids, (Debi 19 and Woody 18) along with my daughter, Kathy (age 13) took to sailing quickly. Scott, age 8 and Erik, age 6 would get into sailing later.

The Penguin was ten feet in length, five-foot beam and carried about eighty square feet of sail area. She was still a centerboard vessel and subject to capsizing. Again, Peggy was not comfortable in this one either. –but we were moving up in size!

Penguins

Scott sorta took over the Snark. He, and a neighborhood Pal even rigged three flashlights for legal 'night sailing'. I don't remember them doing that more than once. –I'll have to ask him about that.

Boating was a lot more relaxed in those days as far as life jackets. Today they are a far cry from what was available; the Kapok-filled, bulky and cumbersome life jacket has been replaced with a compact, auto-inflated or manually activated unit that's quite comfortable and the laws regarding 'wearing' are stricter now.

One-day Peggy asked me that if she helped me with a boat loan could we get something that wouldn't tip over and maybe had a cabin of some kind? We could be partners.

A boat loan was out of the question for me due to my recent bankruptcy. Peggy's financial rating was pristine. I could easily afford my half of the payments but it would be a loan in her name. I agreed reluctantly…it's a 'guy thing'.

We started researching and looking for something suitable. It took close to six months to decide on a model. There were a lot of boat models in our price range. After careful evaluation, we elected to go with a Coronado 25. We

9

would be buying 'used'. Then it took another six months to find the right Coronado 25. We had even gone down to San Francisco, during a three-day weekend, to check one out.

We ended up buying a boat from a Boeing engineer in Everett that, as it turned out, used to work with Kearney, Peggy's first husband. It was in beautiful condition, and fully equipped, including an electric-start outboard motor. We paid $6,500 for it. Interesting enough, with the *"truth in lending"* the total ten-year loan came to $8,800. We had gone from the Snark, at $88, to this new acquisition in a short couple of years. We christened her *"IF",* after our favorite song.

Moorage was found at Yarrow Bay Marina on Lake Washington.

My first adventure as Master-In-Command was taking our new boat from Everett to Bellevue. I did have some help...I can't remember and think it may have been Jim England. I had no idea how long it would take to make that 'trip'. I think it was Jim that suggested that we do it the following day...but "NO", I wanted to get it to our moorage in Yarrow Bay. Jim just sorta shrugged an okay and off we went. Ignorance is bliss, as they say.

It was complicated, that much I do remember. For example, a matter of driving crew up to Everett and then arranging to meet us at our moorage in Kirkland--in between was a long passage on the sound down to Shilshole and then through 'The Locks' and on across the lake. Peggy had volunteered to do the driving part. But then staying up all night waiting to hear from us voyagers. And it took all night!

One can drive from Bellevue to Everett in about twenty minutes. Not so by sea. It was well past late night and well into early morning when we finally made it.

Maybe next time I'll listen to advice from a person with more boating experience. I even sought advice from time to time in this new 'sailing world'.

Woody became my early sailing buddy. We were trying to find out just how the Coronado would handle inclement weather. When the winter storms blew in we'd head out onto Lake Washington and hang on. We did that a lot! We soon learned that the boat could take a hellava lot more than *we* wanted to take. But, we learned.

A funny thing though, now that we owned a boat Peggy and I kinda missed 'shopping for one'.

"IF" the Coronado 25

The Coronado 25's length overall was 25 ft., of course, and had a beam of 8 ft. She carried 309 sq. ft., of sail area. She 'slept' five, had a built-in ice box and room for a 2-burner counter-top stove. We could go cruising!

Arnie Rowe, a friend of the family, crewed with me on three or four trips up north. Arnie was a very experienced sailor and quite familiar with the waters of the Northwest including farther north to Desolation Sound in Canada. (I never made it that far north.)

Mooring on Lake Washington meant that we would have to go through *"The Locks"!* *(*--"Lions, Tigers and Bears, Oh My!")

With Arnie's help and guidance that fearful anxiety was put to bed....but always an adventure with high drama. Arnie was great with the boys, teaching Scott and Erik some of the various nautical knots.

Scott and Erik working on knots

We did Pt. Townsend, Friday Harbor, Bellingham and some ports in between. This was before GPS, which now replaces learning the "ins & outs" of nautical chart reading. I certainly recommend learning chart reading for a back-up, however. And keep in mind there are free or reasonably-priced U.S. Coast Guard courses for 'new-bys '. Check 'em out.

And besides, GPS and the other wonderful digital, electronic devices require 'power'. –and that can take one

12

hellava long extension cord! We have a sail, should the engine quit, but electrical power on a sailboat can be a scarce item requiring batteries. (Always keep one battery rather isolated for a 'Start Battery'.) Learn the basics!

Allow me to suggest that it's a good idea to have an experienced boater around to help learning the ropes of NW cruising. —and besides it's a lot more fun going with other boats. Trust me when I say that any of your friends that have become boaters will be more than happy to offer guidance.

The Locks were built and maintained by the Army Corps of Engineers. Their purpose was to make it possible to 'navigate' between Lake Washington and Puget Sound; the lake being much higher than Puget Sound's 'Sea Level'. ("The Locks" deserve a whole chapter, which we'll cover later.)

Okay, that's all I get for now, over to you Patsy.

FOUR   THE "ANNIE FANNY"
Sometimes called "ZOOM-ZOOM"

Hal did buy a bigger boat, a new 18 ft. fiber-glass runabout, including trailer. She was christened the "ANNIE FANNY" due to her 'flat bottom'. However, I always referred to her as the ZOOM-ZOOM because she was fast; her big engine could get her places in a hurry.

We found moorage in Meydenbauer Bay, just ten blocks from our Bellevue home. With it conveniently close, within walking distance, Hal taught Robin and Ann how to run the boat and carefully 'checked them out'. Ann learned how to run the boat before learning to drive a car.

Both Robin and Ann had friends that lived in Laurelhurst on the other side of Lake Washington. Once Hal was satisfied with their boating skills the girls were allowed to take *ANNIE FANNY* across the lake to visit their friends. It was also handy to zoom across the lake to the UW football stadium for Husky football games.

I asked Hal, "How about Keyport? Can we take the *ANNIE FANNY* that far?" He assured me that it was well within 'the Fanny's' design capabilities.

One sunny weekend the family, including Wolf, climbed aboard and we set a course for Keyport. Leaving Meydenbauer Bay, zooming across Lake Washington to the Montlake Cut, under the University Bridge, Portage Bay, and around Gas Works Park and Lake Union....then the Ship Canal and under the Fremont Bridge, on down to the Ballard Bridge and "The Locks". (The bridges didn't mean anything to us, but Michael's sailboat would be a different matter.)

Lots of pleasure boaters had the same idea of enjoying the day on the Sound and it was a bit crowded. The Small Lock quickly filled. We were directed to the Large Lock by the Lock Master. Hal told me to put out the fenders

14

and he was going to try to inch his way along the side. There was a good-sized Tollycraft that was in front of us and Hal turned and said, "We can tie up next to the Tollycraft, I'll put her on our 'starboard side'". (We're getting so very nautical....)

In the Locks one had to "look alive" and alert—there were many opportunities to hit things, other boats, the walls of the Locks and the gate at the end. In the nice weather there was usually a fairly large audience on shore, watching and sometimes offering advice. It can be quite a show, seeing all the boats, big and small, tied to each other waiting for the water to lower the water down to the level of the Sound, and the gates to open.

Hal reminded us 'line holders' to watch the Lock Master and follow his directions as to when to untie and proceed out of the Lock and under the railroad bridge to Shilshole. All went well. No mishaps this time.

Now we were free to zoom across Puget Sound, around Bainbridge Island, under the Agate Pass Bridge, and on to Keyport.

We arrived at the old dock by the general store where the old **S.S. HYAK** used to dock. The old **HYA**K was a passenger ferry, run on steam, owned and operated by the Kitsap County Transportation Company. It was part of the "Mosquito Fleet" of Puget Sound in the 1920' and 30's. The **HYAK** made scheduled stops at Poulsbo, Scandia, Lemolo and Keyport.

The Puget Sound Mosquito Fleet was a number of private transportation companies running small passenger and freight boats on Puget sound and nearby waterways and rivers. This large group of steam-powered vessels and sternwheelers plied the waters of Puget Sound, stopping at every waterfront dock. Well before the age of Radar and GPS, navigating these waters in bad weather and fog took a high degree of experience. In fog, measuring the time the steamship whistle echo returned from a lee shore could assist in knowing position. An experienced captain needed years of navigation on a particular route to safely pilot his vessel through a fog bank or a dark and rainy night using this method. The need for freight and mail delivery pressed the need for regular schedules. *—the mail must go through!*

The historical period defining the beginning and end of the fleet is ambiguous, but the peak of activity occurred between the First and Second World Wars. The 'fleet' was comprised of more than ten steam powered vessels and a couple of schooners. Only one steamer has survived the rigors of age and progress; the *VIRGINIA V*. She is carefully maintained and chartered for weddings and special events.

The *old* dock at Keyport had not been maintained however and Wolf, eager to head for dry land, jumped out of the boat and landed on a rotten board, breaking it. Down he went, between the boat and the dock—an unexpected dunking. As he came back up to the surface, Hal managed to grab his collar and got his front paws up…Ann grabbed the fur on his back and somehow got this big, wet dog back aboard.

Robin was quick to admonish the Skipper, "Don't stop here again, Dad. This dock has really had it!"

Without further drama Hal steered the boat around the bend into Dogfish Bay. We made it to Keyport.

As I mentioned before the 'cottage' and property on Dogfish Bay belonged to the Crowder family. Mr. and Mrs. Crowder spent summers at Keyport.

When Mr. Crowder passed away, Mrs. Crowder announced that she would not be returning to Keyport. She had no desire to be there without her husband. The Crowder kids kept it in use until eventually it would be put up for sale. My family, having become an extended part of the "Crowder Clan", was able to enjoy its use as well. The cabin was there for the next generation...Barbara, Alice, Bert, Jim and their friends.

When Sheila came to Keyport she remembered the original calendar, still on the wall in the kitchen, years later—always the same calendar with the month and the day Mr. Crowder died. His hat still hung on the hook beside it. Nothing changed.

Often when Hal was out of town on business, I would gather the younger kids in the Love family, Sheila, niece Kathy and nephew Scott (Michael's kids), and head for the ferry and Keyport. Upon arrival I would announce the chores.

"Rake the leaves in front of the kitchen door." The Madrona trees surrounding the cabin were constantly dropping leaves and branches, all of which was a fire hazard....additional chores so each of the kids would be able to participate. There was always plenty that needed to be done.

The kids saved their "chore money" for the nearby Poulsbo Bakery where the many goodies were favorites of the boating community, many who made special trips for the purpose.

I strongly recommend that you include it in your "go to" list when boating. However make note, DO NOT cut across the mouth of Poulsbo harbor...go around the buoy as indicated....there are large rocks under the surface. *READ* that chart! It ruins your whole day when you hit them!

One weekend in late August, my husband, Hal, suggested we tryout our new, fast fiberglass eighteen-foot boat, *ANNIE FANNY*, and go fishing up at Neah Bay. There should be a Chinook salmon run that time of year.

"Girls, do you want to come along?" The answer was an excited, "Yes", from Robin and Ann (ages 16 and 11). Then he explained this was going to be a rough water trip, "Young Sheila can stay with her Godmother."

17

Hal and I knew the ocean waters around Neah Bay. We had brought a disabled cruiser back from the 'ocean-side' of Vancouver Island to Seattle several years before. This time we had a new boat with a powerful engine to master the deep ocean swells.

Hal drove the car and trailered the *ANNIE FANNY* on the ferry to Port Angeles, then drove on up the 'Straits' to Sekiu. We had dinner at the hotel restaurant and stayed the night. The following morning, up at the crack of dawn and a hearty breakfast, we were on our way. We knew to dress warmly….brought caps and gloves for the raw weather to be encountered fishing in an open boat at the mouth of the Pacific Ocean.

Hal drove the trailered boat with all the fishing gear, including 'herring' for bait, to the Neah Bay Indian Reservation. These Native Americans were the Makah Tribe.

The Makah's were fishermen, but were often referred to as the "whale people". Many years ago the tribe would paddle their large canoes out into the ocean to spear whale. The dugout canoes were formed with a high bow, deep sides and big enough for at least six men.

As mentioned in "The Whale People" authored by Roderick Haig-Brown: *"All whaling crews believed that they could succeed in the superhuman task of killing a whale only through the spirit power that came to them through the performance of ceremonial rites."*

The Indian harpooner would make whatever thrusts necessary until the whale turned over and gave up. There was no life left in him. The whole village would share in the bounty of the catch.

We came to the reservation to catch Salmon. We found the boat ramp, backed the trailer to the water's edge, and slid *ANNIE FANNY* into the waters of The Strait of Juan de Fuca.

18

After parking the car and trailer in the adjacent lot, the four of us piled into the boat and zoomed over the waves, the bow hardly touching the water, toward Tatoosh Island. That island is the farthest land west of the Continental United States.

Hal put the boat at 'trolling speed' and headed for the open sea. He handed over the fishing poles, with plug-cut herring for bait and said, "Remember girls, get the feel of the fish bite, then jerk your line to *set the hook*. Hold the line taut as you reel in AND *Hang ON to the pole*—don't let it drop into the water!"

"The water feels a little choppy out here, Dad", Robin said. She was told the waves would be getting bigger. The ***ANNIE FANNY*** rocked back and forth in the big ocean swells. We hung on to the boat for balance, and were getting queasy stomachs.

Ann yelled over the noise of the engine, "Dad these waves are really getting bumpy!"

In the heavy seas, several salmon found our bait, with Robin reeling in the 'first fish'. I stood by with the big net.

All four of us had the chance to reel in a salmon. Robin remembers, "That was an exciting trip." We came home with 'fish in the hold'.

(Illustrations from "The Whale People" by Roderick Hiag-Brown.)

--Michael?

FIVE   THE BALLARD LOCKS

Wikipedia covers in great detail the early planning and construction of the navigable connection between Lake Washington and Puget Sound. In the late 1800's the U.S. Navy endorsed a canal project for the purpose of building a naval shipyard on Lake Washington. Work was started in 1906 by the U.S. Army Corps of Engineers and really got underway under the command of Hiram M. Chittenden. Due to the delays the Navy built the Puget Sound Naval Shipyard in Bremerton, Washington.

Quoting from Wikipedia, the locks were to serve three purposes:

- To maintain the water level of the fresh water Lake Washington and Lake Union at 20-22 feet above sea level, or more specifically 20.6 ft. above Puget Sound's mean low tide.

- To prevent the mixing of sea water from Puget Sound with the fresh water of the lakes. (saltwater intrusion)

- To move boats from the water level of the lakes to the water level of Puget Sound and vice versa.

The system includes two locks. Using the small lock when boat traffic is low conserves fresh water during summer, when the lakes receive less inflow. Having two locks also allows one of the locks to be drained for maintenance without blocking all boat traffic. The locks handle both pleasure boats and commercial vessels, ranging from small boats to fishing boats to cargo ships.

21

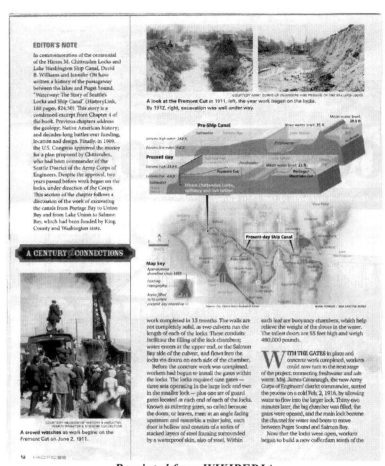

Reprinted from WIKIPEDIA

Over a million tons of cargo, fuel, building materials and seafood products pass through the locks each year.

The complex draws a large attendance due to the beautiful gardens and fish ladders plus watching dumb boaters doing dumb things. A 'featured event' is the last day of a three-day holiday….husbands yelling at wives, etc. One can witness the first stage of divorce or assault in the making.

I've often said that if I was a divorce attorney I would go on the third day just to hand out business cards to angry wives. I'd be a millionaire in a short time. As you can imagine, tempers get short....husbands yell at wives and kids....the Lock Master yells at a particularly dumb boater and the beat goes on.

We all have our favorite "lock story". I'll tell you mine:

At the west end, Puget Sound waters, is a rail road bridge that is mostly in the UP position unless a train is due. If the bridge is DOWN, and it is 'high tide' in the Sound, a sail boater can have a problem if his vessel carries a tall mast. *UNO MÀS* has a mast tall enough to be a problem if those two conditions are present. On the day of my story such was the case.

I was returning from the Sound, the bridge was UP, I was between the bridge and the locks, waiting to go in. The bridge came down, a train was coming. I had been holding position with the throttle against the current of rushing water from the lock opening. When the signal was given to move up into the small lock, I advanced power only to hear the engine starting to speed up as if in 'neutral'....I had either snapped a shaft, or lost the prop. Whatever it was I had lost propulsion.

The boat started coasting back toward the bridge with the still moving current. I yelled at a passing boat, who responded and threw me a line.

He ended up towing me all the way to the yard on Lake Union, through 'the locks' and then the ship canal, the Ballard Bridge and the Fremont Bridge, both of which had to be raised for our tall mast. The yard was where our boat had been taken off the trailer when shipped north from Costa Mesa. They installed a new prop.

THAT's the kinda thing that happens in "boating"...it's like life used to be.

Before leaving this I do want to remind you that one of the reasons my partner and I decided to move up and build *UNO MÀS* was the outboard motor on the Coronado's penchant for quitting when placed in 'reverse'. I'll leave it to your imagination how that played when maneuvering in the locks.

Ballard Locks

The **Hiram M. Chittenden Locks**, or **Ballard Locks**, is a complex of locks at the west end of Salmon Bay, in Seattle, Washington's Lake Washington Ship Canal, between the neighborhoods of Ballard to the north and Magnolia to the south.[2][2][3][4] 5

The Ballard Locks carry more boat traffic than any other lock in the US, and the Locks, along with the fish ladder and the surrounding Carl S. English Jr. Botanical Gardens attract more than one million visitors annually, making it one of Seattle's top tourist attractions.[5] 7—6 The construction of the locks profoundly reshaped the topography of Seattle and the surrounding area, lowering the water level of Lake Washington and Lake Union by 8.8 feet (2.7 m), adding miles of new waterfront land, reversing the flow of rivers, and leaving piers in the eastern half of Salmon Bay high and dry.[5] The Locks are listed on the National Register of Historic Places and the American Society of Civil Engineers Historic Civil Engineering Landmarks.

Chittenden Locks and Lake Washington Ship Canal

U.S. National Register of Historic Places

An aerial view of the locks, facing west

Location	Salmon Bay, Seattle, Washington
Built	1911–1917
Architect	Charles A. D. Young (locks and dam)
	Bebb and Gould (support buildings)
NRHP reference #	78002751
	(https://npgallery.nps.gov/AssetDetail/NRIS/78002751) [1]
Added to NRHP	December 14, 1978

Reprinted from WIKIPEDIA

--your turn Patsy.

24

SIX   HOW TO AFFORD A BIGGER BOAT
On a Shoestring Budget

There are various ways to do many things and we sold the 18 foot *ANNIE FANNY* and bought an older Reinell 28, a wooden cruiser, including a six foot dinghy. We named her the "*LOVE 2*".   We could afford her if Hal followed the advice from a friend who owned a charter service.   "You can have free moorage here on Lake Union if you let your boat out for charter through my charter service."   What a deal; *'free moorage'*.

I drove down to the dock to inspect the *LOVE 2*, hopped on board and checked the layout.   There was a propane stove, a stainless-steel sink and an icebox, molded into the fiberglass cabinet, large enough to hold a block of ice...on the 'port' side.   The "starboard" (right) side of the "salon" (main cabin) was a table with seating that could be converted into a bed.   Behind it was the helm and control panel. One step down into the cabin included two berths and a "head" (toilet).   This was truly a comfortable layout for fun trips and salmon fishing.   But to own it, meant to share it.

Getting her 'ready for Charter' meant that the boat must be washed down, cleaned inside, linens and extra pillows for sleeping.   There must be Emergency flares and life jackets.   Fuel and water tanks filled and a general inspection noting any nicks and scratches.   A 'damage deposit' inventory would be part of the charter paperwork.

This would be a new experience for us.

Our first charter was apparently used as a "party boat".   What a mess!   There had to have been lots of people, lots a booze and careless treatment.   The towels were a mess....they were purchased 'special' for our new boat. New ones were in order—not so fancy.

What are we getting into with this "charter business"? This boat would be chartered for 'cruising' and not for 'partying'. We made that clear to the Charter Service people.

Most people who chartered our boat wanted to cruise through the San Juan's. Often, Hal had to do a trial run Check-Out with the 'charterer', showing the ins and out of running our Love 2. There were those who wanted to charter who had no experience in boat handling, let alone 'chart reading'.

One charterer came with two kids; a boy and a girl, ages seven and nine. The father needed help in more ways than one. Hal asked me to take the kids while he checked out the father in 'basic boat handling' of our *Love 2*. I was handed a shopping list and a blank check. I smiled at the kids and said, "Let's go shopping!"

I drove to a nearby Safeway Store with the kids in tow. We soon came out with ice cream bars and a bag full of groceries. The next stop was the Washington State Liquor Store. (This event took place a few years ago.) While in the store a very nosy middle-aged lady admonished me for "having your children in the liquor store."

I replied to her, "These are *__not__* my children!"

Hal and the father had taken the boat through the Ship Canal and the Locks....I was to meet them at Shilshole Bay Marina. The arranged time and place went okay. The Charterer had learned 'the ropes' to Hal's satisfaction. The kids and groceries, plus the liquor store items were brought aboard. The family was ready to embark.

We said our good-byes and wondered how the father would get along with the kids and boat for the week.

A couple of days later, Hal received a call at his office. It was our charter. The father had found a phone booth on a dock—no Cell Phones then. "The engine is spurting oil. What do I do?

"Where are you?"

"I don't know?"

"Look around you. What do you see?"

"I see a farmer on his tractor."

"Ask him for help. If he has farm machinery, he will know something about engines. –then call me back."

It turned out to be a simple fix. The **LOVE 2** was good to go. Thank you Mr. Farmer!

Father, kids and **Love 2** came back from the week in the San Juan's all in one piece and checked in. Hal looked the boat over and gave the father his 'damage deposit'. Hal could check the engine later. It was a successful charter.

Between charters we had the use of our boat whose primary purpose was fishing. The cruising would be to go to another fishing ground. (You learn where the fish are supposed to be.) Here are some catches and a 'denizen from the sea'.

Jim Crowder & Hal Love with "some fish" well caught....

There were lots of fish to catch in Puget Sound in the 50's and 60's. Salmon fishing became a big interest to Jim and Hal. Summer weekends were divided between Keyport and fishing. Hal and Jim caught fish for great barbecues with enough left for freezing, smoked and canned at the local cannery. The cannery supplied personalized labels.

I liked to go fishing, too.

I remember Hal's instructions on how to catch a salmon. He showed me how to work the fishing reel. (He had already put a 'plug-cut herring' on the hook.)

1. Get the *feel* of the fish bite. Don't reel in on that first nibble. Wait for the second.
2. NOW *JERK* your line in order to 'set' the hook, and start reeling the salmon in.

Hal said, "I'll get the Salmon-Net ready

Sometimes there was another creature from the sea on the end of the line.

I remember another charter incident not so successful. A doctor and wife found a week's charter so pleasant they came back the next year. The doctor felt comfortable handling the boat and his wife equally comfortable dealing with the propane stove and ice box. They only had to bring sleeping bags, fishing poles, a block of ice and food. This time she came with fresh vegetables from their garden and stored them in the ice box. They started out on a trip full of anticipation of an enjoyable, relaxing week.

That was not to be the case!

Hal stayed in his Seattle office during charter periods—just in case something went wrong. Telephone calls from the San Juan's would mean trouble.

The phone rang. The call was from the doctor. "We are having real problems with the engine but were able to put in to Friday Harbor."

Hal answered, "Can you find a mechanic? There must be one close by at Friday Harbor. Hal stood by the phone, no cell phones yet! (Can anyone remember those days of "life without cell phones"?)

The phone rang again. "Hi, I'm Jack at Friday Harbor Marina. I looked the engine over and sorry to say it's 'Kaput', a goner, not fixable."

"Thanks Jack, send me a bill for your service and the serial number of the engine." Hal was able to order a new engine within a couple of days and had Kenmore Air (a seaplane operation) fly it up to Friday Harbor. The doctor and wife stood by while the engine was being installed and then went on with their cruising plans in the repaired boat. We were happy to give them extra days for their inconvenience.

We could have spent a weekend in Paris for 'that one'. Maybe being in the boat chartering business wasn't such a good idea. Shortly thereafter we sold the Reinell.

We were "Boat-less In Seattle".

--Michael?

SEVEN BIGGER BOAT-ITIS

It happens. You've owned a boat for some time and learned all, or most of its issues, and what you wished that you had differently. And you start thinking about your *next boat*.

Oh yes, there will probably be a *next boat*. Anyway, here's how it happened to me:

As I mentioned before, we had found mooring at Yarrow Bay Marina, on Lake Washington. There were a couple of lads that had partnered in the purchase of two boat kits. (Some manufacturers offer some of their models in "kit form".) One was a forty-three foot sloop and the other a thirty-six footer.

Naturally my interest was piqued and so offered some help. I wanted to see how hard it was. I had a lot of time on my hands due to my work schedule. It turned out to be the same kinda stuff; wiring, plumbing…that sort of thing. It was just working in tighter spaces.

My Coronado 25 partner and I had spoken about 'upgrading'. It was tiresome not being able to "stand-up" in the Coronado, having a cabin headroom of five foot six inches. –well, it was that, plus the fact that the 'auxiliary power' was an outboard motor that had the bad habit of *failing* when placed in "Reverse" while we were going through "The Locks". (see "The Locks" chapters) We wanted to be able to stand-up through-out the cabin and also have a permanently mounted inboard engine that would remain 'running' when placed in "Reverse". Is that expecting too much?

Hey, it's only money!

I was personally enthralled with the forty-three-footer but even with the savings of over fifty per cent. the mortgage left was way outta my zone! The thirty-six-footer was in my range.

One of the partners owned a wood products company that specialized in teak. He made his living selling to the boat manufacturers, primarily in Southern California. He told me that one of his accounts, ISLANDER YACHTS, was putting their thirty-foot model in the 'kit market' because it detracted from their new Islander 28 model gaining a high reputation as a cruiser and as a racer.

I ordered a set of plans and instructions created for the kit and discussed it with *my* partner who said, "Let's do it!" He would handle the banking that included the "construction loan" and I felt confident that I could handle and/or 'manage' any subcontracted requirements.

Then surprises of surprises, he went on to say, "Let's buy two, do one and then keep one free and clear." What the Hell, it seemed like a good idea. The order was placed for two Islander 30 Mk II kits.

I still had good connections in the marine industry, from my work with Airmarc. We would be able to buy at discount prices for most of what we needed.

Somehow, the Islander Dealers found out that the "30" was in the kit market and became very upset. The result was that Islander withdrew the model from that market. When they reviewed the orders, they found that we had two kits on order and said that we couldn't do that. My partner said, "I'll handle this. Not to worry."

Well, he did a wonderful job of it. He got our money back for the one kit, a deal on things like a complete wiring harness….already made up…for $15, the permission to contract with Islander's mill foreman and other concessions. It was a hellava deal!

I was working for Kollsman Instrument Company as the northwest Regional Manager. My office was in our

31

home. My primary responsibility was sales and marketing to The Boeing Company, the airlines up in Vancouver, B.C. and United Airlines Maintenance Base in San Francisco. It was wonderful and gave me a lot of free time. For example, Boeing discouraged sales calls on Friday and also Monday. I did manage to stay busy enough to exceed my sales forecast, gave the company their *last* "huffer-puffer" Central Air Data System for United Airlines and aimed the company in the direction of digital systems.

The year was 1975 and our sailboat had just been delivered to Seattle. I had a lot of time to do the work.

With the concessions gained thru my partner's negotiations with Islander Yachts we were ready to move ahead with just the one boat. The manufactured assemblies; hull, deck, Inner liner (The inner liner forms the galley, head, bulkhead locations and forward stateroom), and rudder were purchased and moved about a mile down the road from the Islander factory to a private boat yard in Costa Mesa.

The foreman's quote for the wood bulkheads, wood drawer assemblies and doors, installed, was less money than what I had calculated for materials alone. We accepted his bid.

The boat could be transported to Seattle and placed in the water for further outfitting. This factor saves the cost of '*dry*' moorage at the Yarrow Bay Marina….while we're already paying for a '*wet*' moorage slip, of course. We anxiously awaited delivery. A seemingly long wait was soon satisfied. It was finally here!

Carefully lifting the hull from the trailer and about to be placed in the water we thought it would be appropriate to take this moment to christen her, "*UNO MÁS*". Peggy Lou did the honors. *UNO MÁS* was launched September, 1976.

Peggy Lou christening UNO MÀS
September 1976

UNO MÁS went into the water, her first time, in Lake Union. We filled the diesel tank and 'motored' into, and then across, Lake Washington to Yarrow Bay Marina. More work awaited completion; topside deck fittings, guard rails, wheel steering, galley and head appliances, a three-burner stove and oven, plus a kerosene cabin stove and associated fuel tank. Subcontracted items were mast & boom, interior cushions, depth sounder, 'wind instrumentation', VHF/FM ship-to-shore radio and a stereo system. As you can see, I had a lot to get done. I thought it best to burn some vacation time.

She was finally completed, "fully found", including life jackets. Our sail inventory included Main, Jib and 150 Genoa. Spinnaker Boom, winches and lines were also included. The actual Spinnaker sail itself would have to wait.

Of all the deck hardware the two Spinnaker Winches were the most expensive. The Port winch installed without any problems, however I discovered that the Starboard winch didn't float. It fell into the water. Shocking!

I mean, we're talking about an expensive piece of hardware…very expensive. There was no question, I would have to go after it.

I had done quite a bit of snorkel and then SCUBA diving when living in Laguna Beach, California, and still had my "Dive Card". I purchased a used tank and regulator, purchased a set of fins and asked my neighbor, who had a swimming pool in their back yard if I could borrow his pool to reacquaint myself with the gear. I was ready to dive.

I set about designing a 'vacuum cleaner' since the winch had fallen in the 25-foot part of my moorage…. into the soft-silt lake bottom in this part of Lake Washington.

I had noted that Treasure Divers used a tube with air pressure, so purchased a ten foot section of four inch plastic sewer pipe. I took my air compressor down to the dock and attached the hose to on end of the pipe, squirting up the pipe.

Entering the water gently so as to not stir up the silt on the bottom, and once in place, my crew started the air compressor and I started 'vacuuming' the lake bottom and quickly found the non-floatable very expensive winch. I was surprised to also find an odd assortment of tools, pottery and other items that don't float.

The "seeing" in the lake is terrible. I was used to the visibility in the Pacific Ocean and the severely reduced visibility kinda spooked me. I was uncomfortable. However, I couldn't imagine the need to do this anymore. I was able to recover the cost of the SCUBA gear. It sold quickly when advertised on Craig's List.

UNO MÀS was commissioned October 1st, 1976. We closed the 'construction loan' at $26,200. (At that time the Islander Dealer, out at Shilshole, had an Islander 30 Mk. II in stock, "bare boat", with the sticker price of $46,000!

Not bad, a little sweat and keeping $20,000 in your pocket is a good thing.

SPECIFICATIONS:

Designer: **Peter Finch**   Waterline Length: **24 ft. – 7 in.**
Overall Length: **30 ft.**   Beam: **10 ft.**   Draft: **5 ft.**
Displacement: **8,600 lb.**   Internal Ballast: **3,500 lb.** (Lead)
Hull Speed: **6.44 knots**   Rated Sail Area: **429 sq. ft.**
Mast Height (above waterline): **46.5 ft.***
Main: **187 sq. ft.**   Fore: **242 sq. ft.**
Spinnaker: **758.5 sq. ft.** (PHRF area 180%) Tri-Radial
I = 38.5   J = 12.58   Displacement to Sail Area ratio **20.4%**
Hull Number: **XLYD3002M76L**   Sail Number: **49506**
Washington State License: **WN 0781 JS**

*Bridges: Montlake Bridge   46 ft.
               University Bridge   42 ft,. 6 in.
               Fremont Bridge   30 ft.
               Ballard Bridge   44 ft.

Islander 30, Mk 2. Commissioned "UNO MÁS"
October 1st, 1976

--over to you, Patsy

EIGHT   THE DAGWOOD

We had sold the Reinell cruiser, and were now 'boat-less in Seattle'. It was just as well. Hal had the opportunity to start a new business. The company he had been working for made the move from Los Angeles, CA to Miami, Oklahoma. Hal, with a partner, was able to buy the factory equipment left behind. --- CERVITOR KITCHENS, INC. --- manufacturing small kitchen units. This included sink, stove and refrigerator. The new venture left very little time for our favorite sport, salmon fishing, Hal reflected, "The company never got big, but gave us 30 years of good times."

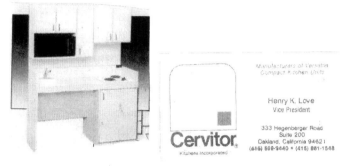

When business partners came to enjoy our northwest, Hal would charter a boat. Someone told us, "It's smarter to charter!" The visitors had to enjoy northwest weather, fog, rain, overcast skies, maybe sun, in order to catch a salmon.

One time Hal and I went on a charter boat to catch that all important fish in San Francisco Bay. As we started out in an early misty morning, cruising out to the ocean, the boat passed under the Golden Gate Bridge, I looked up and saw the huge girders that held the bridge together, and heard the early morning traffic—the cars making the commute.

The tour boat held about 25 people. It was furnished with fishing poles and baited hooks. The fishing line also held a heavy weight ball. I wondered how one could feel the fish nibble with that heavy ball on the line. Somehow I did. Hal brought his own fishing equipment on this trip, and fished the 'northwest way'. Both Hal and I came back with fish, but not so our friend Dave.

Two well caught San Francisco Bay salmon

Fishing out of San Francisco Bay was a different experience.

Several years later, Hal spotted a little 24 ft. wood, "IO" cruiser ('Inboard-Outdrive) in a boat yard. It was while Hal and Jim were fishing in Port Angeles. Hal told me, "Patsy, the price was so cheap I couldn't pass it up, besides, it included a 6 ft. dinghy and a small Evinrude outboard motor for trolling."

It doesn't sound very exciting to me," I answered, "And what is an 'Eye-Oh'?"

Hal explained, "The boat has a big motor in the stern with the transmission and drive outboard. It can zoom up to the fishing grounds in no time."

Inside there was a kerosene stove, sink, small ice box, table with seating and the helm. A step down forward were two bunks that the former owner had made into a double bed...the only redeeming factor, in my eyes.

We kept the boat's original name, "***DOGWOOD***" but I always referred to it as *"Dagwood"* (from the funnies). Hal soon found out why the price of the boat was so cheap. The engine was forever breaking down. The boat spent about equal time between shop-for-repair and the sea. I didn't think it was very reliable, but Hal convinced me that we could have a good time cruising in the ***DOGWOOD***. We did.

The DOGWOOD, Alias "Dagwood".

No fish this one trip. It was time to head home to Bellevue. Hal started up the engine while I put things away in the little cabin, ready for the rough ride home in 'Dagwood'. We were on our way, in the Strait of Juan de Fuca, heading for Pt. Wilson and Port Townsend.

Fifteen minutes out I noticed dark clouds were beginning to gather in the overcast sky. "Hal, the 'Gale Warning Flag' just went up."

Decisions—Do we go back to dock in Port Angeles?

Hal saw a tugboat pulling a barge coming up, (or down) the Strait, and answered, "I can keep going behind the barge. The back-wash at the stern makes a trough that tames the waves." He soon found the tug and barge leaving us behind. We couldn't keep up.

Now I'm seeing bigger waves and white-caps and told Hal, "This is much too rough for my liking." Hal was too busy concentrating on getting the boat through the storm to answer.

The wind had increased creating more stormy seas. Hal was so nervous, his feet were actually doing a tap dance. He was doing his best to keep this unreliable twenty-four footer from being swamped by the building waves.

I didn't want to watch anymore and sat down on the step to the forward cabin.

Moments passed and then I asked, "Shall I get out the life jackets?"

"Yeah", was his breathless response.

I began to pray, *"Hail Mary....full of grace...."*

The boat continued fighting the waves. There was no more conversation until Hal said, "THIS IS IT!"

What did *this* mean? I couldn't see out.

Hal continued, "Point Wilson is just ahead." This meant we were going to make it! The I-O engine held up and didn't break down this time.

The only conversation I remember having on the rest of the trip home was Hal explaining sailboats are better and safer than cruisers, in stormy seas.

In 1981, the Seattle 'dinner hour' traffic was increasing. That summer, when I was teaching at the University of Washington, Hal would pick me up at a small finger pier behind the Fisheries Building in "**DOGWOOD**"; Cheese and crackers plus a bottle of wine, kept us happy while 'cruising' across Lake Washington to our moorage in Meydenbauer Bay, Bellevue, near our home.

Leaving the University, at the Seattle side of the Lake, we could wave at the slow moving traffic…cars crossing the 520 Bridge to Bellevue and beyond.

One planned rendezvous, 5:15 PM, being the appointed time, Hal was not at the dock. An hour later, still no Hal. Perhaps he had stopped to say "Hello" to his Mom. I'll call her. She answered, "Yes, he left here at 4:00 PM."

I waited another hour, or was it longer? I was getting concerned.

Finally, there was Hal…. spotted in the distance, poking along at 'trolling speed' toward the dock. He told me of the engine break-down in the middle of the lake. After several attempts to solve the problem he remembered the old "Evinrude" trolling motor attached to the stern of the boat. He told me, "When I pulled the cord, it started right up." It hadn't been used or even tested since buying the boat.

It was a slow trip back across the lake with what was left of the appetizers and wine. –a great time anyway.

Michael?

NINE WE GO RACING

We made many friends at Yarrow Bay Marina. Sail boaters tend to help each other with various maintenance problems or just hang out together. As the weather started becoming summer, and staying day-light longer we would go for a sail many Friday evenings. It was a wonderful way to 'wind-down' from a hectic week of commerce. Just the sound of the boat moving through the water under wind power was soothing and a best ever form of relaxation. A couple of beers often added to the event.

This evolved into my starting a Friday night racing event. We decided to go from the mouth of Yarrow Bay over to the last buoy in the Montlake channel and then on to Kirkland. It usually took about an hour and a half for that route. Flyers were printed up and distributed to sailboats in our marina as well as those in Kirkland. We soon had a pretty good fleet.

One of the competitors, Bill Mathieson (a well-known NW metal sculptor) asked me if I minded if he tried to get Anthony's Home Port Restaurant, in Kirkland, interested in sponsoring our Friday night "beer-can" races. Bill was successful, but it cost him in that he was to make the beer-can trophies for the various classes.

The course was altered. It now was to start at Kirkland, abeam the restaurant.... then south to Hunt's point, where there would be a real race buoy...then a spinnaker run north to Sand Point, around another real buoy and back to the 'finish' in Kirkland.

The fleet had grown, drawing boats from as far away as Lake Union and Leshi. Bill and I shared the "founders" honors. —an honor that netted us zilch, but we had a lot of fun. Bill has since taken up residence in La Conner, an art colony up in the Skagit Valley where he has his own studio.

Our 'Friday Night Races' were referred to as "Beer-Can" races. In the old days, somebody would throw a beer can into the water and it would become a "Race Buoy". Now it's a little bit more organized, but still just another reason to go sailing.

Looking at it in another way, it is a great learning experience when making the sailboat go where you want it regardless of how the wind is blowing.

Skipper & Executive Officer, Marc Lagen – race night

This doesn't have much to do about 'boats' but you, the reader, might ask, "When did 'Peggy' become Peggy-Lou?" So I'll tell you.

Early in our courtship Peggy and I spent a lot of time watching TV. One day the movie "The Bad & The Beautiful" was playing. There was a scene where Gloria Graham said to Dick Powell, whose movie name was 'James David' something or other, "James David, you have a very naughty mind….I'm happy to say!"

43

From that time on Peggy would frequently call me "James Michael" and I, in return would call her, "Peggy Lou". (Her actual middle name.) It stuck, and she became "Peggy Lou" to friends and family...and remained so to the day that she left us.

When Peggy Lou and I married the partnership on the Coronado became "one". I wasn't really looking for another partner but Jim England said that he had a friend who was looking to get into a sailboat. He made arrangements for us to meet. I'm getting ahead of myself. The chap was Dennis Martin, who owned a company, called 'MONITOR'. The company did computerized freight-payment billing.

We struck a deal.

Dennis had a one memorable experience involving 'single-handed' boat handling in inclement weather. A bad storm came up rapidly. He couldn't get the sails down or the outboard motor started. He ended up getting blown down the lake to Kirkland where the Wawona was moored and struck her. The Wawona was not damaged, but our boat was.

It became a favorite 'marina' drinking story

Dennis took care of it. In the process, we had the hull painted with a new-age paint that had been developed for the Boeing 747. It withstood the extreme temperature range and the expansion and contraction of the fuselage, that the jumbo jet experienced.

We added an ironwood strip and both sides. It looked pretty good, accenting the lines of the boat.

One day I ran into Bob Florence, one of my competitors from. my Pacific Airmotive days. (Pacific Airmotive was an aircraft parts and engine services company. I worked for the Seattle Branch selling aircraft parts in the northwestern states.) At one point Bob had tried to hire me away from PAC, since I was hurting his product sales. That was then, this is now.

We brought each other up to date.

Bob Florence had sold his prior company and now had a new one called Airmarc Corporation. The major product lines were marine & aircraft radios and related avionics.

The Federal Communications Commission (FCC) had recently changed the 'marine radio spectrum' from low-frequency double-side band AM, to VHF/FM (for use up to 25 miles, 'Line Of Sight') and Single Side-band (SSB) for offshore, over-the-horizon applications. Florence, ever the entrepreneur, had decided to take advantage of this newly created market.

When asked what I was doing I told him that I was open to offers. He said why don't I come and starve with him until Airmarc got off the ground. The other folks in the company were taking just enough money for bare necessities; food and rent, etc. He offered me the position of Sales Manager with stock options and credits for the initial efforts. –it was better than unemployment and an interesting industry. And, part of it was in aviation. (I've always loved start-up companies....sometimes one can get lucky and wealthy.)

He did have some aircraft avionics products available. The products were very competitively priced. I still had good contacts in the general aviation market and was able to successfully move enough products to stay ahead of our production rate.

We eventually had a working model of the VHF/FM Marine ship-to-shore radio and it established a good niche in the market. (The Single Side-Band was another story.)

One of the best sales trips I ever had was with Airmarc. We did the New York Boat Show, and then I rented a car and drove down the Atlantic seaboard to Miami, calling on marine electronic dealers, and arriving in time for the Miami Boat Show.

I'm sort of a history buff and it seemed that there was a History Marker every mile. I've always wanted to go back and do that trip again, taking the time to investigate much of the historical sites.

The Miami Boat Show was a huge success and really kicked off our Marine VHF/FM product line. Florence developed a wonderful sales approach for setting up dealers. He had acquired a copy of the Bendix Marine Radio Dealers list. (The old AM radios) Bob then composed a short letter with a questionnaire and freshly-minted two-dollar bills, ordered from our bank. The letter said that the two-dollar bill was to buy a portion of the dealer's time to take the trouble to fill out the questionnaire, the substance of which was "what did they want in a "dealer network". Our return mail was phenomenal! --something like 65% return. Florence wanted to know what the Bendix dealer wanted from the manufacturer as far as policy, etc. Then, of course, he established our Airmarc dealer program accordingly.

And the interesting thing was that when I arrived at a dealership that hadn't sent the questionnaire back...they were apologetic and would point out that it was right there, still in their IN basket.

Our VHF/FM sales were very good but we had an incident with our SSB product. A Marlin boat out of Miami, captained by an owner that had then had a heart attack and his wife couldn't get the SSB to work, he died, she sued.

It was this experience in the boating industry that gave me future access to marine goods at discount and/or dealer prices that was a great help in the building of our Islander 30 Mk2.

Of course today, with the addition of the magic cell phones a lot of boaters forgo the addition of a VHF/FM radio. There are too many things...or variables that can occur boating. Water is not a natural element for 'man' and the U.S. Coast Guard monitors radio emergency frequencies. I strongly recommend having a VHF/FM Ship-to-shore radio 'on board'. For cruising off shore beyond the 25-mile range of VHF, a Single Side-Band (SSB) is essential.

Things at Airmarc took a turn for the worse and it became time to move on. Dennis and I had planned on entering a Saturday morning sailboat race. I couldn't get a hold of him so went ahead and met him at our boat. I told him that I had to work on my resume and wouldn't be able to join him for the race.

Dennis was amazed. He thought that I owned Airmarc. Anyway, he said that he had been looking for a National Sales Manager for his company, MONITOR and would I be interested. We talked about it and cut a deal.

We had offices in Los Angeles, New York, Cleveland and Seattle, of course.

MONITOR had the first IBM System 3 in Seattle. The company got into trouble when a glitch in the IBM hardware caused the system to print 'duplicate' freight payments. It was all recoverable but things came apart very quickly and the company was forced into bankruptcy. Dennis was sued by several of our customers and I was also named in the suit. I was innocent and proved so in court. I was out of a job however, and Dennis couldn't afford the boat payments. My former room-mate bought out his half of the Coronado 25.

* * *

Again, that was then and this is now. With *UNO MÁS* we now had a competitive boat. –back to racing.

We took part in the "Friday Night Anthony Home Port" sailboat races on Lake Washington during the summer months. My crew was essentially unchanged for about seven years. This is almost unheard of. It was probably due to our "strict" rules; *absolutely no drinking until within 24 feet of the vessel...no screaming or shouting at crewmembers or the Captain...and polite suggestions are always welcome.*

The official beverage on-board was "Mickey's Big Mouth" Ale....and since the lid screws back on, your beer won't be spilled when we 'come about'…and PLEASE, no red wine! (--stains horribly.) Very good rules!

Woody became "First Mate"; Jim Tyler was "Chief Of The Boat" (primary responsibility for rigging and handling the Spinnaker). Other members were Marc Lagen, (alternate Skipper, if I was held up at work…pick me up in Kirkland near the 'Start" line.) Step-daughter Debi, Erik, Scott (when in town) and Tom Dorgan, plus his 'squeeze', Roxanne. Other occasional members became "Able-Bodied", "Grinders", *Mickey's-fetchers,* and other tasks as they occurred. By and large, it was a well-coordinated and efficient crew, with the one exception of an incident related as follows:.

The Islander really liked 'heavy air'. Friday summer evenings on Lake Washington did not provide much of that but one night it did. I couldn't believe it, I not only had a great start but also was graced with heavy air. We were *sailing* and *leading* the fleet to the first mark.

Well, this one night with our kind of wind, we arrived at the first mark ahead of the race fleet. In our surprised excitement, during the attempt to raise the spinnaker, we lost the halyard….it got away and went to the top of the mast. We quickly got the Bos'n Chair out…started to hook up the Jib Halyard to the chair….and *that* halyard got away to the top of the mast. We only had the Main Halyard left. God help the crewmember that loses that one! So we lowered the Main sail, attached the Bos'n Chair and sent the most recent culprit up to fetch the two halyards that were flopping around up near the mast top.

In the meantime…the entire fleet came sailing by with hoots of laughter and 'raspberries'. We finally got halyards and sails squared away, the spinnaker flying and took off in pursuit.

We finished DFL. ("Dead *Frxxking* Last!)

However, Lady Luck smiled at us and we were awarded a trophy for "Perseverance"…and here she be.

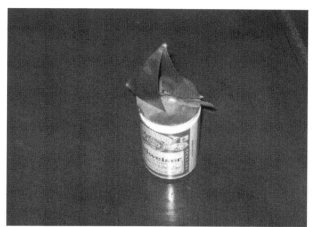

Beer Can Trophy awarded to *S.V. UNO MÁS* for *"PERSEVERANCE"*

As I mentioned earlier, the crew had really shaped up and very enthusiastic about our Friday Night Races. Mark Lagen was my Executive Officer and had been instructed to not wait for me, or any other crew member, not making it to departure time. We had a 'secondary' time and place at a Kirkland Park dock near the Start Line for 'stragglers'. It was one of those times when I was the 'straggler' and Lagen followed orders and took the boat out.

He had made a good start and was holding a good line when a SWAN 40 came barging past, ramming the side rather brusquely and *UNO MÀS* began taking on water.

Mark immediately headed for Yarrow Bay Marina, where I had finally arrived and was able to arrange an immediate 'haul-out'.

The Swan 40 skipper was very apologetic and took care of everything. So, a word of advice; If you're going to get hit, pick a bigger and richer one and make sure you're "in the right". –it worked out just fine, we made the next race after a week of repair work.

There were many more races that summer and the following summers as well. The Friday night races were a great way to wind down from a hectic business week and were enjoyed by all.

Our 1994 Press Release:

UNO MAS COMPLETES 1994 ANTHONY'S HOME PORT SERIES

Kirkland, WA: The Islander 30 Mk II, ably commanded by James M. (Mike) McEniry, has successfully completed the Anthony's Home Port Friday Night Race Series.

His Executive Officer, Erik Robinson, assisted in all elements of strategy and crew discipline. Unfortunately he was unable to make the last race. This was due to staging a final stand battle with the "Dragon Lady" and her pimply-assed son! —the latter was last seen hiding under his mummy's skirts!

Tom Dorgan, Chief of the Boat and Sail Trimmer, did an excellent job throughout the series, only missing two races due to conflicting schedules.

Debi Robinson Cole, Port Winch and Spinnaker Flyer also missed a couple of races, one of which was the last race. She came to the assistance of her brother, Erik, in his battle with the Dragon Lady and her cowardly son, missing the last race. Debi was very reliable throughout the series, gaining more and more experience as the season progressed.

Roxanne Love served in the capacity of Starboard Winch and 'galley rat' in this, her first season. She will certainly be asked back next year.

James Tyler, or 'old reliable' as he is referred to by the salty crew, again served in various capacities; fore deck, strategy, sniveler, but is most famous and appreciated for his culinary achievements...especially the smoked chicken! As a cook and able deck hand, he'll always be welcome aboard.

Mark Nuss, gave what little time that he could spare. It was rumored that he will not be back next season. In fact it has been reported that he won't even be missed.

Lon Alsman, a famous jazz bass player, tried his hand at crew for the first time this 1994 season. It has been said that he is a great bass player. Given enough time he might make a decent crew member. However, he was always entertaining.

The skipper, Mike McEniry, and co-founder of the popular race series said that all it would take to be a contender is about $10,000. Who knows? —it could happen!

-30-

...your turn Patsy.

50

TEN   BIG TROUBLE AT THE LOCKS

It was late in the summer, one of the last weekends in the season. We were coming back from Keyport in our new, 28ft older boat, the *LOVE 2*. As we approached the Locks, Hal reached for the controls to put the boat in 'Neutral'. There was no response. There was no response in 'Forward', or 'Reverse', either... oh, oh. It appeared the controls had become disconnected from the gear box. How are we going to get through the Locks without controls? And, then on to our moorage in Lake Union?

The situation called for some quick thinking and quick action. Hal began to shout directions, "Patsy, get the fenders out and be ready with the Stern Line. I'll let the boat drift over to the pilings to tie up outside the Locks."

As the boat neared the pilings, I could reach for one. Hal turned off the engine and was able to get to the gear box and the rod that controlled Forward, Neutral and Reverse. "Ann," Hal said, "This will work if you sit on the floor and move the gear rod in Neutral, Forward and Reverse as I give directions. Try it."

Ann got in place and tried, "I can move it three ways, Dad."

We waited for the Locks to open and the rush of water to empty into the Sound, and watched the Dock Master direct the boat traffic leaving the Locks. People on shore watched, too.

This busy Sunday afternoon the big Locks were being used. More than twenty-five small boats would have to maneuver into position and tie up to each other. Could Hal control our boat, giving Ann directions from below? When the Dock Master motioned us to come, Hall asked, "Ann, are you ready to work the gears?" Ann gave a nod in answer. Hal started the engine and yelled "Forward". Slowly Hal eased the boat between two others. "Neutral", Hall called out. The boat drifted into position. It was working!

I looked down at her, this 7th Grader doing an important job of working the gear shift.

I handed our line to the boat handler next to us, and she tied it to their cleat. The same procedure went on the other side. When all the boats were secured, the Lock door closed, and the water level began to rise to the lake level.

We did get through the Locks with Ann at the shifting controls, and on to our moorage. We secured and unloaded the boat...piled into the car and headed home. By the time Hal drove into our driveway, the family exhausted from a day in the sun and weary from out two hour adventure at the Locks.

Great job...well done, Ann.

Your turn, Michael.

52

ELEVEN   CRUISING

As mentioned in a prior chapter, my good friend Arnie Rowe came along with Scott, Erik, and me, to share his knowledge of the Northwest waters. We did Pt. Townsend, then on up to Friday Harbor and all around Whidbey Island, including Deception Pass. Arnie pointed out to me that to transit Deception Pass one should know about tide flow. I didn't ever see it but Arnie said that certain tide flow conditions can cause a hefty 'whirlpool effect' strong enough to cause boats to founder.

The family early cruising was in the Coronado 25. We learned basic planning, provisioning, and dealing with a 'camping lifestyle'. Essentially you learn from others. It helps if you get to know someone with a boat and you are nice enough of a person to get invited.

So we come to the 'where to go' part of cruising. Our moorage slip would take a thirty foot boat. It was our first, and initially for the Coronado 25. The moorage was in Yarrow Bay, on the east-side of Lake Washington, a little south of Kirkland, near the east end of the 520 Floating Bridge. Mooring on the lake made it convenient for 'day sailing'. The late summer daylight hours in the Northwest provided many an evening for a beautiful warm summer sail, –and when accompanied by a full moon, a spiritual event. Our home was an easy ten minute drive from our marina. Some of my best sailing memories are of those summer evenings on the lake…and the moonlight sails especially.

There is a lot of friendly banter between 'sail-boaters' and 'power-boaters'. The primary difference is in the intended use of the boat. A power-boater wants to get to a destination quickly, and in the case of my Sister's family, the fishing grounds. A sail-boater's intention is to enjoy, sometime relish, the process of getting there. The quietness and peacefulness of sailing is almost a spiritual experience.

TOP, Erik Robinson, Scott McEniry, Peggy Lou, Debi Robinson & her brother, Woody Robinson; taking their turn at the helm.

54

Conversations with friends bring forth the opinions of the non-boaters where statements of "—Sailing is way too much work", or "I just want to relax, have a beer and drive."

Sailing is not a 'lot of work' unless you're racing. And that isn't so much work as learning how to tweak a little more speed out of a sail trim or using wind direction to fine tune a desired course. There are 'sailing clubs' offering classes in sailing techniques and should be considered. I was lucky; I had an "Arnie". He taught me how to trim the sails for a 'balanced helm'. By that, I mean one could then sail "hands-off". Arnie had learned his skills crewing a serious 'race boat'. But you only need to *do all that work* if you need to hold a true course. On a large body of water like the Lake or the Sound, you have room to set a sail basic trim and go open a beer.

Speaking of which, the 'official' beer on our race boat was Mickey's, Big-Mouth, a 6% malt liquor in a barrel-shaped bottle with a large screw-on lid. This enabled the "in-biber-ed" to screw the lid back on before *'coming about'* thus preventing the spilling of all of the drinks. The Seattle area is known for its Micro-brewers and many of my crew complained about Mickey's but then agreed that it becomes an 'acquired taste'. —sorta like learning how to drink Scotch.

It isn't a good idea to have hard liquor on board. Boating, in general, encourages relaxing imbibing. Oh, a bottle of Rum or Brandy for cold winter sailing is okay, but not on race-night. Red wine is not allowed for other than 'at-moorage' dining…certainly not while 'under way'. (It can stain white fiberglass when spilled.)

More than one race-night found the icebox full of Mickey's when several crew members each brought a six pack. I believe that I pointed out one of our Race Rules was that there would be absolutely no drinking until within 24 feet of the boat!

Okay, but this is a chapter about cruising. We have determined that our cruising would be on Puget Sound and north into the San Juan Islands. That doesn't mean that there aren't places to go and to see in the south area of Puget Sound. In fact one trip south to Gig Harbor was memorable for two reasons that I'll share with you.

It was a weekend 'over-nighter' and I don't remember why we chose Gig Harbor. The entire family was aboard **UNO MÀS**, our Islander 30 Mk 2. We arrived and looked for a decent place to moor and was pleasantly surprised to see one open on the end of a dock. We couldn't believe our good fortune until about 2:00 o'clock in the morning when we were awakened by the boat leaning over about thirty degrees...the tide had gone out. Only our dock lines prevented us from going over farther. It was a long night.

Debi, Peggy Lou and co-author Michael

The following morning, and once again afloat with breakfast out of the way we headed north up Colson Passage up the inside of Vashon Island. We had a brisk southerly wind and saw close to ten knots on the Knot Meter! Let me tell you ten knots on the water in a thirty-foot sail-boat is a real ride! Most of our cruising is in the five to seven knot range.

In fact, when leaving our Yarrow Bay moorage for a cruise I would enter into the logbook "time under power" and "time under sail". Once cruising the Sound and, if under five knots, I would start up the 'iron wind' (engine). Reviewing the logbook over a couple of years disclosed about equally *half* the time under power and sail. I'll add here that I did have to refill the 30 gallon fuel tank every other year whether it needed it or not. "Golly gee".

A lovely weekend "go to" sail was/is, out through the Locks and a left turn to go across to Bremerton (don't turn early...go all the way out to the buoy before turning southwest; it shoals a bit.) and then, by-passing Bremerton, up the inside passage of Bainbridge Island to Poulsbo. Tie up at the Visitor's Dock and go up to Front Street NE, turning left and down to the middle of the next block, will find you at "Sluy's Poulsbo Bakery. Engorge! --for 'sail-boaters' there are no calories! (Well, that count, anyway.)

Another favorite trip was Roche Harbor on San Juan Island. And a couple of times, our trip continued from Roche Harbor, on around north of Orcas Island and over to Bellingham.

Growing up in the Northwest, I'd always had an interest in boating of all kinds. As I said earlier, I was pushed into 'sail' due to fuel costs associated with operating a power boat. I soon became enamored with the spirituality of sailing...the quietness, peacefulness bringing on a total relaxation experience. High on the 'feel-good' list is the blending of the forces of Mother Nature's winds and harnessing of that wind to go where you want to go. And it is the "going" that is more important than the "getting there". It has been noted that when a 'boater' goes down to his boat he decides where to go. When a sail-boater goes down to his boat he/she is where he wants to be. *Patsy?*

TWELVE   DON'T ROCK THE BOAT

Our Girls were grown, married and had families. Now the next generation came cruising with us. Jenny, John and Steve had fun playing in the dinghy taking turns at rowing close by. Hal told them, "Take short strokes, don't dig the oars in too deep.

One time I saw all three kids stand up at the same time in the dinghy causing it to rock violently...to the point of capsizing. My heart was in my mouth as I shouted, "STOP. ALL OF YOU SIT DOWN! --you are rocking the boat!" I envisioned all three kids, ages seven, eight and nine, dumped in the water.

Kids, it is time to talk about safety rules when out in the boat.

1. Always wear your life jacket.
2. Learn to swim.
3. Learn to row.
4. Put the oars in the boat when not in use. *'Boat your oars.'*
5. Fasten boat lines SECURELY to a cleat on the dock.
6. Be careful when beaching the boat,; you don't want to damage the bottom.
7. In a small skiff or boat, to change places, one person stands at a time.
8. Be aware of changes in the weather while out on the water.
9. MAN OVERBOARD ---What to do---Never take your eyes off the person in the water. Let someone else rescue, by throwing a life-ring or an oar, or anything for the person to grab.
10. Listen to the Captain; follow his direction. He will tell you how to handle the lines, where to put the fenders when docking. Remember, STERN FIRST when docking—be part of the crew.

As the grandkids grew older, they learned to drive the skiff/outboard by themselves and steer the cruiser. They looked forward to sleeping in their sleeping bags on deck. Most of all, fishing and crabbing. They learned how to pick up live crab without being pinched. The grandkids had fun off the boat as well as on—combing the beach for shell and rock treasures—checking the tide pools for the purple starfish.

Here's an easy way to trap a crab, albite 'old', since it requires a lady's nylon stocking…. does anyone wear them anymore when boating?

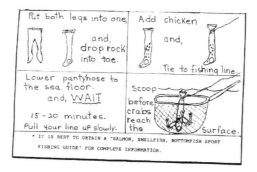

Anyway, it really works…. especially if you don't have some fancy, expensive Crab Traps, or you had left them on the dock. Remember, you only keep the male crabs. (Throw the females back.)

--Michael?

THIRTEEN   LET'S TALK BOATS

I've tried to share with you, the reader, what this phenomena of "boating" is all about. It's expensive, bothersome, whether the boat is kept in the water or on a trailer, and trying to justify usage vs. cost.... by the hour is a lost cause, so what's it all about?

My boat partner used to have a sign behind his desk that said, "If it Flies, Floats or *cuddles*, Rent It". At that time he also had an airplane and another boat and had recently married. (I wonder what ever happened to that sign...)

Well, anyway, I think it's part of our primeval urges to do something, or go somewhere...it's locked in to our DNA. There's a body of water.... what's on the other side? How do I get there, I can't walk...they hadn't invented swimming yet, so let's grab a log and invent boating! It is just my opinion, I don't mean to preach. But think about it, somewhat like 'camping out'... dealing with the elements, the satisfaction of exploration and selection of the vehicle.

I believe that I mentioned in a previous chapter that a part of the mystique is the shopping and selection of model, size and function. It's fun learning about the "boating thing".

For me, I was sorta 'nudged' into sailing, having seen firsthand the relationship of the throttle-to-the-Fuel Gauge. I couldn't afford hundred-dollar weekends. So, then it just became a matter of learning how the sail-thing works and learning how to appreciate the stress relief of the Zen-like peacefulness of a sailboat sailing across a body of water, under wind driven sail-power.

It's right up there next to *nirvana*!

An evening sail under spinnaker....

Some days are just better than others. And then there are the times that are 'golden'. Life can *be* 'golden' at times, creating cherished memories.

Sure, it's expensive. I'm not going to try to hide that but I'll point out a comparison to the cost of a shrink or the heart attack of a young "Type A" individual.

And, Hey! Let's not forget that the IRS recognizes it as a 'vacation cabin', and the mortgage payments are deductible. Oo-Rah! (I believe that it has to be able to *"eat, sleep and provide basic hygiene facilities,"* to qualify.)

I must apologize for this babbling on about sailing. I wish I had the skill to convey the feelings and life-changing experiences that were given to me.

I think I'll leave it at that for now.

--Patsy....

FOURTEEN THE TOLLYCRAFT

The 28 ft. "TOLLYCRAFT" was our next boat. I liked the 'trawler design' with a wide, blue/turquoise stripe. Hal bought it from a fishing buddy. We could afford to own this boat without having to charter it out.

The interior was typical.... sink, propane stove, counter, on the port side, and built-in table/dinette seating, with the helm on the starboard side. There was a step down to the cabin/berths and head. The boat was just right for fishing and family outings. We named her "*LOVE 3*".

We decided to keep *LOVE 3* in Port Angeles where there was still good salmon fishing. Besides, we liked the town. Moorage for our power boat was less expensive up here on the peninsula. Hal found a floating boathouse that would protect our wooden "Tolly" from the weather. The fella, whose boat was in the adjacent boathouse, had an old refrigerator. I asked, Is this where you keep the salmon you caught?" He laughingly replied, "Oh no, that's where I keep my cans of beer!"

28 ft. TOLLYCRAFT

It was the summer we bought the Tollycraft. With family on board, we headed toward Port Angeles and the new 'boathouse moorage'

"This boat is easy to handle", exclaimed Hal, "It cruises so smoothly." --that was until the boat took a huge wave made by an impolite boater passing by at high speed. The 'Tolly' bounced, lurched and rocked. Before I could get to the casserole sitting on the counter, I watched it slide off the edge and land upside down on the floor. −lid broken. Tomato sauce oozing out, followed by onions, green peppers, mushrooms, etc. −with smells of garlic.

"Oh Yuck!, what a mess! Where do I start the cleanup?" It was a lesson learned. Next time put the casserole in the sink when traveling.

Our girls, Ann and Sheila, helped clean up the mess...with smiles on their faces. They knew the family would be eating dinner at the Chinese restaurant that night instead, and that would mean fortune cookies for dessert!

That casserole mess left a lasting memory.

BACK TO FISHING

I remember Hal's instructions on how to catch a salmon.

1. He showed me how to work the fishing reel. He had already put a 'plug-cut' herring on the hook.
2. Get the feel of the fish bite. Don't reel-in on the first nibble...wait for the second bite.
3. NOW, JERK your line to set the hook, and start reeling the salmon in. Hal said, "I'll get the salmon net ready."

One time, fishing in Port Angeles, I felt a strike on my line. I followed Hal's instructions, and started reeling the salmon in. This fish was a real fighter. My pole was bending and the line, taut and jerky. This must be a big one. As the fish finally surfaced I could see what was happening.

I had a salmon on my hook, and at the same time, a tussle with a seal who was taking a bite out of the salmon's tail.

I won!

--fish ON!

The 'Tolly' took us to other northwest waters besides Port Angeles. One weekend we headed for Poulsbo and Keyport with the family. The stop in Poulsbo always included "Slys' Bakery and coffee. Even the day-old donuts were good.

On to Keyport, where Hal anchored out in Dogfish Bay. The kids took turns rowing the little skiff to the beach.

Grandson Dylan fished off the Tolly. "I caught one, a dogfish." AS he reeled it in, the tail of the 'spiny' variety of dogfish scraped the skin off of Hal's arm.....ouch!

One of the kids rowed me in to the beach and I went up to the Crowder cabin and got a rake and bucket. Clams were usually plentiful. We could have steamed clams with garlic bread for dinner. On one visit to Keyport, Mr. Crowder told us, "You won't find many clams today. The other night, when the tide was out, the Indians came with gunny sacks, helping themselves to the bounty of the beach. The 'Treaty' gave them rights."

Bert Crowder remembers, --the beach included 'geoducks' (pronounced 'gooey duck'), a giant clam that dug itself deep into the sand and mud, leaving a small hole behind. If you stepped on its hole, the geoduck retaliated with a powerful squirt. The geoduck could dig faster than we could. "They were hard to catch."

He went on to say, "They were much tougher to eat than the Butter Clams that abounded at low tide, anyway."

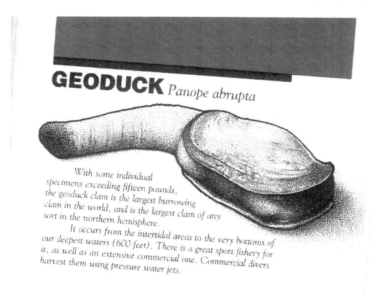

GEODUCK *Panope abrupta*

With some individual specimens exceeding fifteen pounds, the geoduck clam is the largest burrowing clam in the world, and is the largest clam of any sort in the northern hemisphere.

It occurs from the intertidal areas to the very bottoms of our deepest waters (600 feet). There is a great sport fishery for it, as well as an extensive commercial one. Commercial divers harvest them using pressure water jets.

Port Angeles was a logging town with a paper mill in the 1970's. The ferry '*COHO*' (Black Ball Transportation)

Black Ball's Ferry, *THE COHO*

had a route straight to Victoria, British Columbia. Port Angeles was a "Port of Entry" – Customs.

HISTORY: Settlers began arriving in the 1850's. In 1862, Abraham Lincoln designated 3,520 acres in Port Angeles as a Federal Reserve on which to build a lighthouse and establish military presence. The Coast Guard Air Station on Ediz Hook was built later in 1935.

While Hal and friends were fishing, the girls and I would take the ferry over to Victoria for the day. Port Angeles was a 'fun' town.

Daughter Robin at the helm

One winter, in the 1980's, the Pacific Northwest experienced a big snowstorm, dumping six to ten inches of heavy wet snow. Traffic in the whole area came almost to a standstill. The snow was so wet and heavy, small boats could sink from the weight of so much snow. Our 'Tolly' would be okay because the floating boathouse was giving her protection from the elements.

Then the telephone call came from the manager of the Port Angeles Marina, "Your boathouse is beginning to sink…it has about a foot of snow on the roof."

OUR BOAT IS INSIDE!! It would be sinking, too. We couldn't drive up to Pt. Angeles to take care of the situation. The marina manager went on to say, "I can get help here to shovel the snow off the roof, is that agreeable to you?"

Hal thought, "Do we have a choice? An additional $100 was added to the expense of owning a boat that winter...."

Hal Love, inside the boat house with 'Tolly'

Michael, next?

FIFTEEN   A BLUNDER

I'm not trying to "top" your story Patsy. But I think I will. –and I didn't have a choice either.

It all started on Tyler's birthday. Another crew member and I decided to make it an event since Tyler had done a great job running the fore-deck. As "Chief-of the-boat" it was his responsibility to manage the crew in handling and flying the Spinnaker. Their efforts during the last race season had led to our only Race Trophy. And besides, his wife had asked me to keep him away until she could do her somewhat elaborate surprise-party preparation stuff.

Tyler & Author, Mickeys's in hand, with the Author smoking a KOOL

We decided to go across the lake and over into Lake Union to a restaurant, with a bar and that had a dock. We had a few cocktails, and then a couple more, before sailing back to our moorage in Yarrow Bay. A "Whiskey Front" had rolled in.

At that time, *UNO MÀS* did not have a 'Holding Tank' installed and pumped ship's waste overboard. (highly illegal now) There is a small inlet valve on the lower side of the toilet that prevents water from coming in to the bowl. If that valve is left in the 'open' position the water will rise in the bowl to about two or three inches from the top rim of the bowl…. that being equal to the water-level outside the boat.

Part of my routine, in securing the boat, is to check that valve 'closed' and then to "arm" the mechanical Float Valve that actuates the Bilge Pump. Well, when I bent over to insure the inlet valve was closed, I damn near passed out. I might not have closed it all the way. Anyway, it was open enough for water to come in and fill the bowl to about three inches below the rim.

Later that evening, on March 1st 1989, it snowed. And then it snowed some more…a heavy, wet, ten inches of snow. The weight of the snow lowered the boat below the 'about three inches', and water came into the boat. Even with my loss of attention, due to drink, I had "armed" the Bilge Pump's Float Valve that would activate the pump if incoming water moved the float up.) Well dear reader, the float valve was 'gucked-up' with crud and the float didn't move 'up' to activate the bilge pump. The eight-dollar float valve had failed. *UNO MÀS* had sunk in the slip and was hanging on her mooring lines.

70

A never forgotten sight. A real *"Oh drat!"*

UNQ MÀS 'hanging' on her mooring lines!

It was going to take more than a day or two to make things right. The first thing was to get the 'water' out of the boat.

The marina crew suggested that they bring their tug in to the slip next to mine, bridge over to the dock and then get a couple of straps under the boat, and winch it up far enough to get the coaming (hull rail) up and out of the water.

It would then be a simple matter of putting a high-velocity pump aboard and pump the water out of the hull.

Once dry, **UNO MÀS** was floated over to the marina dock and lifted out of the water to be worked on. The insurance folk looked everything over and declared all interior items a 'complete loss'. Starting with headliner, curtains & rugs, cushions, VHF radio, stereo system, wind & depth instrumentation... everything but the diesel engine. The contamination of diesel oil was heavy throughout the boat.

I had always admired the interiors of sailing yachts like the very expensive Hans Christian Models. Essentially, they had teak & holly cabin sole, tongue & groove planked over-head, with teak crossovers on four-foot centers with knobby things on each end where the crossover meets the sides. They had green, plush, mohair upholstery, brass fixtures, brass lamps, and lots of teak. We already had the lots of teak in our bulkheads and galley trim, doors and drawers. I was determined to replicate that 'stately interior.' It would be like a "Gentleman's library", suitable for 'brandy and a good cigar'. I got quotes for the "replace with new" items and used that money for the Teak & Holly cabin sole, the overhead planking, and two brass hanging lamps. Use of my labor was applied to new brass electric cabin lights, curtains and the teak 'cross-overs'. A ship-wright contractor was found that understood what I was hoping to accomplish. He installed strips for attaching the 'planked overhead' tongue & groove.

--planking the 'over-head'

He then installed the Teak & Holly cabin sole. I asked how much he would charge to do the six 'knobby' things that would be on each end of the 'teak cross-overs'. He said $400. I felt that was a bit high and thought I could do 'em. I bought some Styrofoam blocks to make patterns, since each one would be slightly different. I worked for a couple of nights on the FIRST one...still hadn't gotten anything but a pile of Styrofoam sawdust. The following day I called the contractor and asked if his offer of $400 was still good. Laughing, he replied, "Sure, okay".

Teak & Holly cabin sole

The 'finished look'

The cushions and curtains were ready for installation. The interior was beginning to look like a real sailboat. I was proud of the results of my efforts. We had lost a summer of sailing but **UNO MÀS** looked better than new!

--the finished look, with 'knobby ends'

Finally, she was finished. I called my partner and arranged to meet him at the boat.

He arrived, went below, carefully looking around then slowly turned to me and said, "Well done, McEniry, well done."

--Patsy?

SIXTEEN

THE BIG FISH

It had been a beautiful day for cruising with a few clouds against the blue sky. We anchored for the night in a quiet little cove behind Protection Island. I made 'Tomato Basil Chicken' for dinner with left over banana cake for desert. Hal settled down with a good book. He had caught a salmon earlier.

I decided to try fishing one more time that evening. With pole and baited hook in hand, I dropped the line to the ocean floor. Then walked slowly around the stern of the boat while dragging the line along the bottom.

"Hey, there's something down there….it feels like a nibble."

"You probably snagged an old shoe."

"No Hal, it feels like a real bite." I started to reel in. "Whatever it is, it's heavy."

Coming up to the surface, I could see a big codfish on my line. —it measured 42 inches long. "Wow! What a thrill… grab the salmon net!"

It took the two of us to haul this big fish into the boat. The salmon net bent to the weight. That fish ended up being 'smoked' in Kirkland. The Smoked Cod was a real treat for family and friends.

Looking around for some more material for this writing, I came across one of our Log Books. The following are a few excerpts:

9-25-84 Leave *PA, (Pt. Angeles) 0701AM Fished Dallas Banks till 12:30PM. Engine making a 'tappet noise', overheating—leak in the shaft aft of G box (gear)—some oil in bilge water*

10-19-84 *Riser leaking---installed new risers. Should we name boat "Gumperson's Law IV?"*

5-26-85 Gas *at Shilshole. Depart at 9:07AM. Pass Pt. Wilson 12:07PM. Fished short time at Dallas bank—fog closed in tight. Dungeness Buoy—up & down fog till near Port Angeles. Found #66 boathouse. Dinner, cards—sleep onboard. Next day fog cleared. Went out around Ediz Hook to fish. Got up to Crown Mill (rough) and discovered we left fishing poles in the boathouse!*

***P**atsy's 42" codfish...Hal's well-caught salmon.*

6-21/23-85 *Sunny and windy all trip---Gale & small craft (warnings) each day. Fished briefly 3 mornings –one evening at low slack tide---one good hit, 2* *dogfish. Patsy caught one silver---good meals, good trip, Like the boathouse.*

9-23-85 *Happy Wedding Anniversary in Port Angeles.*

1-1-86 *Depart Port Angeles for Seattle, returned in one hour—too rough.*

3-1-86 Trip Log, PA to Seattle
Leave PA alone 9:30AM –calm, good visibility---Dungeness 9:53AM---clear, strong 'rip'---Wilson Buoy 11:33AM----Pt Hudson, 11:53AM---Bush Pt, 1:16PM----Point No Point, 2:35PM---Apple cove Pt., 3:11PM-----Kingston, 3:30PM (refuel)---Locks, 6:15PM, moorage at Stimson Marina, Seattle 7:00PM. **TIME: 9.5 hrs.**

Here's another one that might be a little more interesting. I call it "Happy Anniversary".

9-23-89 *We left the dock in Bellevue at 6:45 AM –went through the Locks, refueled at Shilshole (86 gallons). The Weather was crystal clear. We were looking forward to cruising to La Conner for an 'anniversary dinner'.*
At Applecove Point the boat's engine was missing badly. Change of plans, and headed to Pt. Wilson instead. The boat broke down completely five miles northwest of Pt. Wilson. The engine stopped running.

"I can't get any RPM's", Hal yelled. "We're right in the middle of the 'shipping lanes'." I could see a huge container ship in the distance coming toward us. Hal decided it was time to call for help from the Coast guard. That container ship will be on us pretty soon.

The Coast Guard response was, "Are there people whose lives are in danger?"

Hal answered, "Well, our boat has broken down, and we are stuck in the shipping lanes. And I can see a large container ship headed this way."

Hal was transmitting to the Coast guard on our VHF/FM radio. −someone had heard the conversation and cut in, asking, "Do you need a tow?"

A commercial towing company in Port Townsend listens to Coast Guard 'distress calls'. Soon a tugboat from the towing company came to our rescue, and towed our boat to the Marine Repair Dock in Port Townsend. −the bill, $190. I thought that would be the price of a *"VERY NICE"* hotel room (1989). Happy Anniversary... oh well.

Hal, ever the gallant gentleman, suggested, "While the boat is being repaired, let's take a bus to Port Angeles and stay at the Red Lion Inn. Tomorrow, we can take the ferry "COHO" to Victoria and have a nice dinner at our favorite restaurant, 'Chauney's '." --I liked that plan. "Maybe the boat will be repaired by the time we get back."

It took a little longer than anticipated, and on the 27th the 'Tolly' was good to go. The parts for the engine had come and were installed. After sleeping on board. Hal got up early and went across the road to MacDonald's and brought back our breakfast. "If we get an early start we can do a little fishing on the way." --Hal's favorite pastime.

--next

SEVENTEEN A FISHERMAN SHOWS US
SAILORS HOW TO FISH

Uncle Hal, my sister's husband, offered to take my boys fishing. Since I wasn't a "fisherman", it was kind of him to take the time and effort. My two youngest, Scott and Eric, (ages 10 & 7) were excited and anxious to go. We would take the boat over to Shilshole in the evening after the vehicle traffic subsides on the bridges. It would be an early departure from Shilshole after Uncle Hal arrived. After an early dinner Scott, Erik and I drove down to Yarrow Bay Marina, on Lake Washington, and we would have to motor across the lake, and under the Montlake Bridge, then through Lake Union and under the Fremont Bridge…. the Ship Canal and under the Ballard Bridge to the 'Locks' and under the railroad bridge (hoping that it would be 'up') finally over to Shilshole and moorage for the night.

As was our habit when transiting the Ship Canal, we'd stop and say hello to my former High School classmate Bob Newman, better known as "Gertrude" on the J.P. Patches TV show. He was a favorite of the boys. Bob lived on a houseboat on the Ship Canal. —he said something like *'drop a fish off for his dinner, on our way back'.*

We finally cleared the Locks, and Lady Luck was with us; the Railroad Bridge was in the 'up' position.

We motored on over to Shilshole Marina, found a spot and after mooring went up to the office to pay for the 'overnight'.

It was "Zero-Dark-Thirty" the following morning when Uncle Hal arrived at Shilshole marina and rousted the sleepy crew. "Up and at 'em" came the call, to ready the boat for our exciting day of fishing.

Uncle Hal had brought poles, a net and bait for the boys. I would merely be just the 'Skipper'…driving the boat

81

to wherever Uncle Hal dictated…and then 'trolling' per instructions while the crew fished. I had frequently told Hal that, "I eat 'em, I don't catch 'em!"

Uncle Hal with Scott & Erik

Even though Uncle Hal was an experienced boater, we reviewed the Emergency Procedures used aboard UNO MÀS so he would know our routine.

1. If a "Man Overboard" is called out, THAT person was responsible for never taking an eye off the person in the water.
2. Throw cockpit cushions of either side of the boat. (Don't try to stand up and throw a cushion to the person…just get it in the water!)
3. I reviewed Engine Controls with Hal, since he would assume command if I was the one in the water.
4. If under sail, douse the sail and start the engine for recovery efforts. Return and pick me up, please.

Hal directed me to head for Point Wilson for our fishing effort. We ate hard-boiled eggs for breakfast on the way. I was going to put some bacon on to fry but even though my stove was gimballed it was too rough so I forgot about it. The eggs were filling and the boys wanted to fish. Patience is not a virtue of the young.

Upon arrival at Pt. Wilson I re-assumed command and reduced the engine power setting to a suitable trolling speed. Hal handed out the fishing poles and baited hooks and started teaching the boys this "fishing game". I steered the boat, avoiding other fishing people, and stayed out of my crew's way.

It wasn't long before the excitement started. Scott got a 'first-fish' on. Unfortunately, it was a dogfish and a throw-back. It wasn't too much later when Erik yelled, "I got one!"

Hal started coaching him.... "Let him take the bait, now give a jerk to set your hook, I'll get the net. Keep slowly reeling in, Erik."

It was a salmon. And big enough for a family dinner at home tonight. His Mom, Peggy-Lou, would be proud. Scott, ever the gentleman, congratulated him, adding that he had gotten "first fish".

Uncle Hal made a few attempts and did catch something but it was also a 'throw-back'.

I drove the boat.

Apparently there is 'fishing' and then there is 'mooching'. Uncle Hal told us the difference. It starts with a 6-to-18 pound line....a 2-to-8 ounce Sinker....4-to-8 feet of 6-to-18 pound line to a Swivel, and then 1-to-3 feet of 6-to-18 pound line....and finally to a "Plug-Cut" herring. Got that? The purpose is to get the line down deep enough to find the chinook salmon, where it lives.

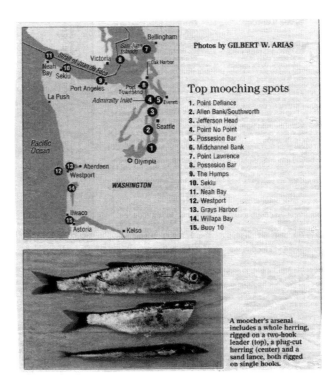

Photos by GILBERT W. ARIAS

Top mooching spots

1. Point Defiance
2. Allen Bank/Southworth
3. Jefferson Head
4. Point No Point
5. Possesion Bar
6. Midchannel Bank
7. Point Lawrence
8. Possesion Bar
9. The Humps
10. Sekiu
11. Neah Bay
12. Westport
13. Grays Harbor
14. Willapa Bay
15. Buoy 10

A moocher's arsenal includes a whole herring, rigged on a two-hook leader (top), a plug-cut herring (center) and a sand lance, both rigged on single hooks.

Mooching Map

The fishing now over I headed the boat up into the wind, turned the helm over to Hal, saying just hold her here until I get the sails up. Scott and Erik, ever the trained lads, handled the lines. I made my way back to the cockpit, took over the helm and set sail for Shilshole.

Uncle Hal was delighted. He said, "This is fun, it's something to do *AFTER* we get through fishing!"

Co-author & Henry King Love, alias 'Uncle Hal'

The sail back to Shilshole and Hal's car, was indeed a lot of fun…. The wind was good and the sound of the hull slicing through the light chop was a wonderful reward to this first 'fishing trip'.

So much not said.

--Patsy?

EIGHTEEN   THE JUDGE BOLDT DECISION

On February 12th, 1974, Federal Judge, George Boldt (1903-1984) of the Ninth Circuit Court, issued a historic ruling reaffirming the 'fishing rights' of Native Americans.

Western Washington tribes had been assured the right to fish at usual and accustomed grounds by Federal treaties signed in 1854 and 1855.

By 1970, Washington State now had a law that regulated ALL FISHING in the Salish Sea and beyond. The Tribes defied that law, stating their right to fish according to the 1855 Treaty.   ---Case, United States vs. Washington State Tribes.

Judge Boldt held that the government promise to secure the fishing for the Tribes was central to the 'treaty-making' process.

DECISION: Fifty percent of all fish caught goes to the Native Americans, and the other fifty percent goes to nontribal commercial fishermen. A small percent of that goes to the sport fishermen.

The Boldt Decision revolutionized the state fisheries industry and led to violent clashes between tribal and non-tribal fishermen and regulators. In 1975, the Ninth Circuit Court of Appeals upheld Boldt's ruling, and in 1979 the U.S. Supreme Court largely affirmed it. Principles established by the Boldt Decision have since been applied to other resources, including shellfish.

The late 1960's and early 1970's saw the diminishing of the salmon runs to the rivers to spawn in the northwest waters.   There were just fewer fish... the reason that

Washington State felt the need to change regulations for fishing.

Hal felt the Judge Boldt's Decision percentages should be readjusted.

Captain Henry, and fishing family Ann & Robin

Another Trip To Catch The Elusive Salmon

"Let's head up to Neah Bay," Hal suggested. The weather was right, and there could be salmon coming into the 'Straits'. We drove to Port Angeles and stayed overnight on the 'Tolly' in the boathouse, then cruised up the 'Straits' the following morning. The seas were calm and the sun was shining through a bit of fog. By the time we reached the lonely lighthouse at Cape Flattery, fog had really settled in, with only a few sun breaks. Hal found a protected place to fish and Ann, Hal and I set our poles to fish off the stern of the boat.

"Watch my pole while I check the head." It wasn't long before all three fishing poles were bobbing up and down. Ann started reeling her fish in, "It's not a salmon."

"It's bass," I yelled, "I think Ann caught a bass, Hal."

"Oh-oh." Hal knew what was happening. In the fog the boat had drifted too close to the rocky shoreline. Bass like a rocky habitat. He rushed to the wheel, started up the engine, and moved the boat away before big waves could send us crashing onto the rocks.

We ended up catching a couple of salmon... one of which slipped from my hand as I was cleaning it off the side of the boat! What a loss! I remember thinking it might as well have been my wrist-watch. In fact, I would have preferred that it had been my watch that fell into the water. Salmon are scarce these days.

--Michael?

NINETEEN   A REFLECTION

When researching for this endeavor I stumbled across an old 'Photo Album' that my mother had put together. In it are several pictures taken aboard their sailboat called the *"ANEMONE"*, plying the waters off Catalina Island, California. The date is 1925

The grainy, faded pictures do not do justice to the event.

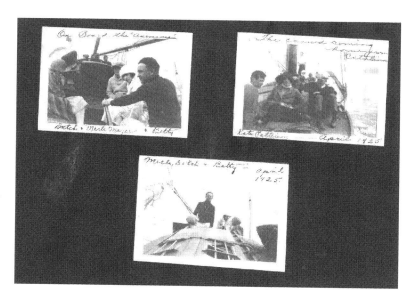

From a few other snapshots I was able to determine that she is about a 35 to 38 foot, 'gaff-rigged sloop'. My mother has told me that they took quite a few trips over to Catalina Island. Some of them more exciting than others. The worst, for her, was fog…. and sometimes some pretty large waves. I remember reminding her that it *was* out in the
`   Pacific *Ocean!* --twenty-six miles out in fact.

So the "McEniry" boating experience started, in 'modern times' anyway, in 1925. Patsy and I felt it warranted including a poem that our Mother wrote during that period.

THE PELICAN

A wonderful bird is the Pelican,

His beak can hold more than his belly can.

He can hold in his beak,

enough food for a week,

But I don't know how in Hell he can.

Betty Marie Braga-McEniry
(1903 – to- 1987)

Over to you Patsy.

TWENTY   FOR SALE

The "FOR SALE" sign caught Hal's eye as he walked the marina docks one sunny day. It was in the window of a wood power boat, trawler design—ten feet longer than our Tollycraft. He liked the classic look and decided to see the inside. The salesman at Wolfe Marine Sales gave a quick tour, including a few particulars. Hal thanked him and said, "I may be back."

At dinner that night, Hal brought up the discussion of the boat he saw at the marina. Choosing his words carefully, "It is a sturdy wooden boat… and has already been to Alaska and back, Patsy."

I'm thinking, *'Is this a case of "boat-it-is disease" again? --a bigger boat in our lives?'*

"But we already have a boat!", was my initial response.

"You could just go look at it," Hal answered.

We did. What impressed me, on our walk-through were the two real 'porthole windows'. I did wonder why the boat had two 'heads' (toilets), I later found out two heads on a boat were handy when the one head plugs up.

This time the salesman gave Hal the official listing write-up.

Exterior – This is a custom designed 38 ft. power boat, designed by Ed monk, Sr., Naval Architect. Her beam is 13 ft., 6 inches. She was built in 1966 at Nordland Boat Works, in Tacoma. The covered back deck is enclosed by canvas, a 'Flying Bridge', with helm, is over the Main Cabin, as is the dinghy (a Hylaker, by name) and its davits. And a 'walk-around' deck.

91

Interior – Forward Cabin has a "V" berth with storage underneath, and a hatch in the overheard. There is a vanity, sink, shower and head with a gear locker. Steps lead up to the main salon, or Main Cabin. The Salon has an 'inside helm' forward, a settee (that makes a double berth) and a table. The Galley includes deep sinks, refrigerator and a diesel range which runs off the "Detroit" diesel engine fuel tank and also warms the cabin.

I had questions about cooking on the big, iron top stove with oven. The salesman remarked that it was a '*slow cooker*' ...taking a half a day to cook a potato. –meals would have to be organized to fit *that* problem, I thought.

The SHALEX, soon to be re-commissioned ECHO SUMMIT

Hal read more about the inner working.... the machinery, single-screw propeller...cruising speed and the many extras. We then took a 'trial run'.

That night, Hal presented his case for buying the boat. "Patsy, now that we're living in a townhouse, there is less maintenance at home, and more time for boating. In fact, this boat could be a 'live-aboard'. Besides, the boat runs on diesel, much cheaper than gas. The salesman said the fuel tank only needs filling by the season!"

I could tell that Hal really wanted this boat. So we bought it. Now we have two boats.

"There are three of life's possessions that
Are almost indispensable, each entailing
A major investment.
There is a home, a car and a boat.
The car is, in modern life, a necessity, the
Home also, and to give up the boat is
Almost un-thinkable".

Ed Monk, Sr., Naval Architect

So, a FOR-SALE sign went into the window on the Tollycraft.

A note in the Ship's Log – Boat to Dick Wrights "Boat Bottom Shop" for 'haul-out & survey', to sell it to the next customer.

Regardless of all the breakdowns on the 'Tolly', we had lots of good times on that boat.... the many cruises to Port Angeles, Poulsbo (bakery stop) and on to Keyport with family.... fond memories of fishing off the 'Tolly'.

And now Hal is looking for "covered moorage that'll take a thirty-eight-footer".

Now we go fishing & crabbing in style

     I'm broiling salmon for supper, using my husband's recipe:

"HENRY'S SALMON SECRETS"

1 ea Tbsp   Butter
2 ea Tbsp   Lemon Juice
Dash Worcestershire Sauce
Dash Onion Powder
       Brown Sugar
       Salt & Pepper
Melt butter, add other ingredients for basting, (less the brown sugar)   Cook for one minute. Baste the salmon, sprinkling the Brown Sugar.
    Now ready to broil or grill.

     We decided to change the name of this beautiful 'Monk trawler' to *"ECHO SUMMIT"*, and also installed a new stove.

The covered back deck and large cabin Salon will provide plenty of room for family and guests.

Taking possession of the soon to be commissioned **ECHO SUMMIT** currently at the Lake Union marina we started looking for moorage.

--next?

TWENTY-ONE   A DELIVERY CRUISE

My son, Scott, was working as a yacht broker in Bellingham. He knew that I was between projects and had some free time and called, asking if I would like to ferry a boat down to Seattle for a "Boats Afloat" boat show coming up soon. It sounded like a fun thing to do so I jumped on it. Hey! --any excuse to get out on the water.

The boat was a Hunter 336, The Hunter line of sailboats were very up-scale, beautiful things and sold well despite their high cost.

It would be quite a trip; well over a hundred miles from Bellingham to Seattle, then through the Locks into Lake Union to the show site. At least ten to twelve hours.

I met Scott at the Seattle Hunter Dealer's moorage and left my car there, driving up to Bellingham the following morning with Scott. After a thorough 'check-out' in the workings of the Hunter 33, I was able to depart Bellingham about noon.

Due to 'time constraints', this trip would be under power. I guess we could call it "boating". It's probably a "primeval" thing, commanding a conveyance and making it go where *you* want to go, arriving un-hurt and able to use the conveyance again. It's a feel-good.

Clearing Bellingham Bay, I headed south through Padilla Bay and into the Stillaguamish Channel that runs through the town of La Conner, a quaint 'artist's colony'. In fact, as of this writing, it is the home of my sister, Patsy McEniry Love, and the co-author of this literary effort. Put La Conner on your "Go-To" list, by land or sea.

It's getting dark out now but I'm still comfortable in my planned route and a first time in Saratoga Passage. I should add that this is all before GPS, relying on actual "chart reading" and such. (*Why in my day...heh-heh.*)

Things look different at night, but the road signs are well-lit buoys. I'm logging "Command Night Hours" now approaching Possession Sound and the City of Everett. I'm in familiar waters finally. (Reference Chapter Three; bringing the Coronado 25 down to Kirkland from Everett.)

Now it's a simple matter of avoiding cross sound ferries, rocks and other boats, including the larger container ships plying the north-south Ship Channel.

Here's an easier-to-read map of the general area that I covered ferrying this beautiful, new, luxurious yacht to be displayed at the upcoming "Boats Afloat Show". Stuck at the helm for most of the whole trip, I didn't have much opportunity to enjoy the luxury.

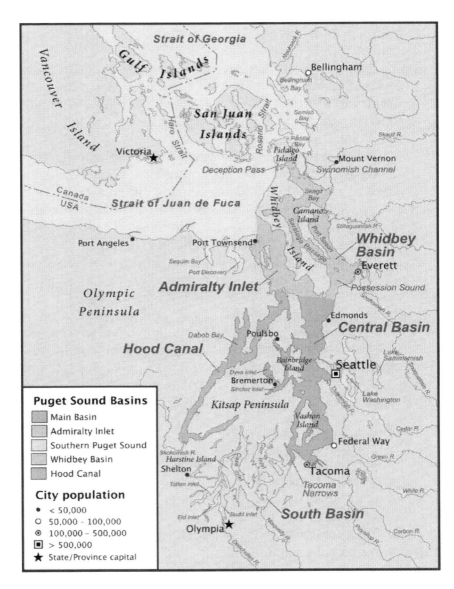

Finally made it. T'was a very long day…and night. Dropped the keys where previously directed and headed home. –a wonderful experience.

Researching for this effort, I came across some Logbook entry writing sent to me by my son, Scott. His descriptions of things like anchoring, sail-set decisions and general seamanship factors are well stated, giving the reader a feel for the type of things encountered when cruising in a sailboat.

As I have stated in earlier chapters, I had the good fortune of an "Arnie" to show me the ropes and places to go. However, he took me to places that had docks to tie up to, relieving me of the responsibility of 'anchoring out'.

I'm going to add here a few of the Log Book entries mentioned: (I have taken the liberty to shorten up some of the entries.)

LOG of *IANTHE,* August 2006
Scott McEniry – Skipper
Liam McEniry – Crew (age 9)

After a late start, Liam and I finally had all provisions, supplies, sea bags, and accoutrements aboard. We had moved *IANTHE* to the work-dock to facilitate loading, and after eating dinner, we cast off at about 1800. (6:00 PM) The boat was a disaster below, but we ignored it as we motored across Bellingham Bay over a calm sea with little wind. We steered for Inati Bay, determined to have that be our initial 'overnight'. WE pulled in at 2000 (8:00 PM), to a fairly full bay. We finally decided to anchor on the south side. It quickly became apparent that the log boom was too close for comfort, so we changed our location. Satisfied with the second 'set', we set about putting the boat to rights. With the radio on, Liam and I spent an hour organizing our living space. Heading topsides to check our anchor set, I was alarmed to find that the log boom was kissing our bow! I had thought that it was tied firmly to shore, but evidently, it was not. Hauling the anchor up yet again, we reset towards the entrance to the bay, far from the rest of the crowd, and there spent a very rolly, and not very restful sleep.

In my over twenty years of sailing I have never 'anchored out', since we didn't have a dinghy. –back to the Log.

The next day, we upped anchor and headed south towards Carter Point. We were enroute to Rosario, on Orcas Island, to meet up with our friend Dan Drake and his son, Chase. We raised main 110 Geneo, and soon saw 4 knots on the GPS. The wind was west at about 10 kts, and I decided a sail change to the 150 was in order. We soon were averaging 5 kts as we beat towards Viti Rocks. We tacked and headed for Vendovi. After tacking, I roused out Washburn's Tables, and discovered we'd be fighting a 2.5+ knot current for most of the day. The wind started to die, and after two more tacks, we were barely making any headway; the GPS registered 0 kts too many times to mention. Dousing the headsail, the 'iron wind' came on and carried us past the south end of Sinclair. Once in Bellingham Channel, the sails were raised and averaged 6 kts to Towhead Island, where the wind dropped off entirely. With the sails stowed, we motored across Rosario, the current pushing us almost a mile to the north of our course to Obstruction Pass. Finally, out of the adverse currents, we made good time to Rosario. We grabbed a buoy at 1730 (5:30 PM) with the aid of Dan and Chase in their inflatable. It was blowing hard, so the extra help was greatly appreciated. We had a fun evening and tumbled into bed at 2330 (11:30 PM).

The following day we decided that Rosario would be a fun place to hang for the day. Liam got some rowing practice in, learning the ins and outs of dinghy handling. It didn't take him too long to master the task, and pretty soon he was rowing figure eights between the boat and a convenient dock. He was quite proud of his abilities, and decided that he really liked rowing.

When you stay at Rosario, you have the run of the grounds, including access to both the indoor and outdoor pool. Liam insisted on rowing us in and took a spin around *IANTHE* and then the scenic route through the anchorage, eventually arriving at the dinghy dock. We headed for the pool, where we spent the day soaking up the sun, being joined by Chase, Dan and Linda. After getting thoroughly sunburned, we headed back to the boat for some appetizers, and then over to Dan's boat for dinner.

The following morning, we rowed in for another swim and some ice and headed back to the boat around 1100, We made our farewells, slipped our moorage and headed south out of East Sound, bound for Fisherman Bay on Lopez Island. The wind, which had been blowing nicely for the past two days, decided it had worked hard enough, and we motored over calm seas. Liam practiced identifying landmarks from the chart, and proved to be quite competent. We threaded the entrance to the bay and tied up at the Islander Resort dock. We walked up to the Lopez Creamery, a gourmet ice cream maker and had desert before dinner. We strolled back to the boat, stopping for ice at the store (most sailboats have an "ice-box" not a fridge), which was really expensive. In fact, everything there was very expensive, and there were none of the usual boater's amenities, such as a garbage dump. They even charged for showers in the locked pool area. Rosario was a much better deal. We went back down to the boat, fired up the oil lamps and played a couple of games. I taught Liam how to play Poker and now don't have to pay him an allowance until he's 17.

Continuing on our voyage we pointed our nose north, our destination Sucia Island. We had timed our departure to take advantage of the incoming tide, which would push us up San Juan Channel past Jones Island, the north shore of Orcas and on into Sucia. Four hours of steady motoring at a sedate pace was enough time to cover the twenty-two miles to Shallow Bay, where we dropped the hook at around 1430 (2;30 PM) We were comfortably secure, and it was time to head to shore for the much vaunted, and much anticipated "caves of Sucia Island". The island has a long and varied history. The Salish tribes used it as a summer camping ground, as shellfish and salmon were plentiful, but they were frequently attacked by marauding Haida tribes from further north. Sucia's name is Spanish for "dirty", as it is surrounded by nasty, bottom-ripping reefs that are invisible in all but the lowest of tides. The Spanish explored these waters in the 16th century, and many of the islands, channels, and straits still carry their names—Strait of Juan de Fuca, Matia Island, Eliza Island, just to name a few. Vancouver explored the area in the 18th century, and is responsible for naming most of the rest bits of rock that make up the San Juan Archipelago.

But what Sucia was most famous for was its sandstone caves on the shores of Shallow Bay. None are exceptionally deep, but most are eminently suited for hiding all kinds of things; people (in the case of Salish hiding from attackers), smugglers of Chinese laborers being brought in for cheap labor, and booze from Canada during prohibition. And more recently, treasures for kids to find as they explore the caves and fissures of the cliff.

All in all, a memorable time spent with my son Liam, who was soon to become a 'sailor' in his own right.

Patsy?

TWENTY-TWO   MOORAGE

A bigger boat in our lives meant bigger moorage and fees. Stimson Marina in Seattle was a bit pricey. We were told La Conner was a good place to moor your boat...... less expensive, and the gateway to the San Juans, and great for crabbing. The area was not new to my husband, Hal, and me. We had been guests on a boat trip there in 1958, right after the "Rainbow Bridge" was built.

We headed north in the '***ECHO SUMMIT***', through the Ballard Locks on our way to Victoria, making a stop in La Conner. Hal tied up to the guest dock and went to the marina office, inquiring about permanent moorage. He was told the marina was full, with a 'waiting list'. But, the Dock Master said, it was possible to sub-lease for six months at a time, making one's own arrangements with the different owners.

After two years of sub-leasing, Hal was able to get permanent moorage in the north marina, and happy that it was under cover. Our older wooden boat needed the extra protection.

It was a beautiful location, abounding in wild life. We saw seals swimming between the finger piers and boats. Shaggy crested kingfishers flew near, screeching as they perched on old dock pilings. I watched a great blue heron stand motionless, ankle deep in the water across the channel, then strike out suddenly at prey below the surface. At night, when the lights of the marina came on, we would hear those regal birds as they swooped down and landed on top of the marina roof with a loud 'PLUNK'. There, they could survey the lit waters below for little fish. One night, our cat watched a heron strolling the dock...right past our boat. It was walking slowly, stealthily, one big foot after another. We watched the heron with curiosity. The cat kept her distance from that big bird.

While Hal worked on maintaining our boat, I became acquainted with the town. I drove across the "Rainbow Bridge" and volunteered at the Swinomish Indian Reservation "Head Start" program. (Work that I had done in my civilian endeavors.) Later, I joined 'Friends of the La Conner Library' to see if we might retire in this area.

The La Conner Marina, in the 1990's allowed 'live-aboards'. We became part of that community, as we were driving up to the valley from Bellevue, spending fifty percent of the time on our boat. There were potluck parties on the dock every holiday with this diverse group of singles, retired couples, and families with children. One little preschooler had every water-toy made. The 'live-aboard' community even included an ordained minister. Dogs and cats had a home on the boats, too. It was a good life.

One Father's Day, the Dock Master came to our boat with a Father's Day card.... mailed from our daughter, Ann. How did the card get to the La Conner Marina? Hal was so pleased, his Ship's Log read, "I shed tears... it was cool". La Conner, with less than a thousand population, was a friendly town.

I remember one big celebration on the docks. –a wedding. It was a sunny day, perfect for the event. We were all invited. The bride wasn't dressed in white/veil, but looked radiant and lovely for the occasion. The ordained minister performed the wedding ceremony on the stern of the couple's forty-five-foot sailboat. Their reception was set up on the dock with a big wedding cake and champagne. We toasted the happy couple... how romantic!

One-year Hollywood came to La Conner to film a movie. ("The Fugitive") A store-front was changed on First Street to fit the plot. They shot some scenes at a house up on the hill by the Methodist Church, and other places. Some night scenes were filmed near the north marina. Strobe lights were placed on high poles across the channel from our boat. We could see all the action, including a stunt actor falling off the dock into the water. A local boat owner was hired to be in his skiff as a rescue boat, ready and watching nearby. The filming went on until 4:00 AM. We stayed up 'til the end, not wanting to miss a thing.

One quiet, rainy afternoon in the marina, a couple had recently sold their boat and the gal was cleaning and filling boxes to take to the car. Their fiberglass boat was two long docks away.

"SPLASH" --I heard a big splash, followed by a loud cry of "HELP". It was a woman's voice. I was some distance away. I needed her to know she was heard by someone. I yelled, "Help, someone needs help," and started running towards 'H' Dock. Hopefully, someone else had heard the shouts. As it happened, two men were working on a boat not too far away and came to her rescue. The woman had slipped on her wet, slippery swim-step while carrying a big box.

There were other times when people and things fell into the water at the North Marina. My husband, Hal, jumped off the side of our boat onto the 'finger pier, not regaining his balance and fell in between the boat and the dock. I watched him fall, and in a flash, got to the dock to help, fearful of injuries... *aghast!*

Luckily his friend Ed was there to help him out, saying calmly, "Can you pull yourself up 'til your elbows are on the dock?" Hal could do that. Then, Ed reached for Hal's belt and pulled him up the rest of the way. Hal made it up on the dock, wet and disgruntled. He was okay, disgruntled and very wet.

There were no ladders attached to the docks for safety.

In another incident, my wallet fell out of my purse and into the water. Hal and I decided it was important enough to warrant hiring a diver. He found the wallet and other interesting items, as well.

Our marina community had many stories. On our starboard side was a nice-looking sailboat owned by a couple of fellas who came down often to check it out and wash it down. We had friendly chats on the subject of the sea. ("Sea Stories?) One fella talked about his former job as a professional diver.

His story:
"I worked for a diving company that researched shipwrecks in the South China Sea. The company made a deal with the government of the Philippine Islands to split any bounty. Two wrecks were located. One was the Spanish galleon "San Jose". There must have been a big storm where the crashing waves had caused the ship to end up on a reef near Lubang Island in the early 1600's. Its cargo was 'blue and white china'." He went on to say the dishes were just medium quality.

The other shipwreck was in the same vicinity, and had a cargo of beautiful china porcelain with many pieces intact. Some of it is displayed in museums. The fella brought pictures to show me.

I asked him, "Did you ever keep anything you found from the shipwrecks?"

"Oh yes, there were lots of small pieces of shard that washed ashore after typhoons over the centuries, from the Spanish Galleon, 'San Jose'."

I told him I would *LOVE* to have just one small piece, in exchange for a jar of my blackberry jam.

The next time I saw the fella on his sailboat, he hailed me. "I have something for you," and handed me a plastic sack full of blue and white shards from the wreck. I was thrilled. Those dishes had been down in the deep for centuries. The prize was worth several jars of blackberry jam.

That's not the end of the story. After the treasure was found and recovered from the two shipwrecks, the Philippine government reneged on the agreement. The diving company received nothing and went bankrupt.

Later, I found a 'National Geographic' map "Treasures Of The World", Lost and Found. There it was, the shipwreck of the "San Jose", sunk off Lubang Island in the Philippines, in the early 1600's.

ECHO SUMMIT was ideal for family cruising and crabbing. Salmon were getting scarce so we looked into crabbing.

Remember, 'keepers' have to be male...

Our salon was big enough to accommodate large groups. Babies ate in a box. Grandchildren were old enough to handle the lines and help in the maintenance.

Robin's Dylan, swabbing the deck.

Baby-inna-box!

Uncle Mike came aboard and joined in on the fun.

"I like to eat crab," he said. "Others can catch 'em."

He stayed all night, sleeping on the couch in the salon that included his own facilities (head). He told Hal he would have to get used to the noisy diesel engine while underway. He was used to cruising with the 'wind in the sails'. (He actually admitted that when cruising he was under power half the time.... when lack of wind slowed the boat to less than five knots he would fire up the "iron wind".)

We eventually decided to just move to La Conner and purchased a nice two-story home, on Fifth Street, in town.

After ten years on the docks there were big changes. Live-aboards were no longer allowed, then later accepted with higher moorage rates. All moorage rates took a big jump.

Not too long after, we sold **ECHO SUMMIT** –a reluctant good-bye.

She had given us fifteen years of good cruising and good times. –indeed, a 'reluctant good-bye'.

your turn, Michael

TWENTY-THREE   MORE SAILING

There came a time to 'think about' selling UNO MÀS. The racing season was over. Fall was upon us. For some reason my son Scott thought that the boat should be up in Bellingham where he was working as, or for, a Yacht Broker. Okay, it seemed like some kind of plan and another excuse for a long trip. I alerted the crew for those who would like to make the trip and we put a plan together...like moving my VW van up to Bellingham for bringing the crew back to Bellevue. We decided to make it a two-day trip, with an RON ("Remain Over Night") in Port Townsend.

We arranged sleeping accommodations with Debi and Roxanne Love (no relation) up forward in the Vee berth, Scott and Erik in the Main cabin upper and lower bunks (the back of the main settee folds up, forming the top bunk, leaving the bottom as a berth.

When the back cushion of the short, port settee is removed, it reveals an opening in the bulkhead that allows one's feet to extend through the bulkhead and under the sink in the Head.

Woody decided to join us at the last minute and he would be sleeping out in the cockpit.

It was a "Full Boat".

We arrived at Port Townsend earlier than we thought possible, so decided to press on to Roche Harbor. For some unknown reason, it was 'party time' at Roche Harbor. My crew pulled "Liberty" and somehow, during their "Rape Pillage & Burn" activities, managed to avoid the 'constabulary', making a clean break of it.

Leaving Roche, over the top of Orcas Island and almost a straight shot east to Bellingham. That straight shot run was some of the best sailing ever done aboard UNO

MÀS. –we *screamed* into Bellingham Bay, at close to 10 knots!

All seven-crew climbed into my VW bus for the long drive home. –a really great trip!

A month or so later Scott suggested that I move the boat back to Bellevue. I forget the reason why.   Anyway, Tom Dorgan and Roxanne Love said that they would make the trip with me.

A few words about Tom and Roxanne. First of all, Tom and I worked together and he sailed with me on a couple of Friday nights and asked to become part of the race crew. Roxanne worked with my Step-Daughter Debi and came along a couple of race nights. She eventually asked to become a permanent part of the race crew. Both Tom and Roxanne were married to other people. They ended up falling in love with each other… divorced their spouses and are still together to this day. They're now living in Florida, doing internet computer work in order to be able to live anywhere. I still get a Christmas card. (I don't know if they ever married.)

Our planned route back would take us through the Swinomish Channel that goes right by La Conner. I told Patsy that we would be coming by. She and Hal were on the **ECHO SUMMIT**, that weekend, not having purchased a house in La Conner yet.

When we arrived, Hal rowed out in his dinghy and took the following picture. It wasn't too long after that Scott, still in his position as a yacht broker, sold **UNO MÀS** for me.

I thought the next picture would be appropriate for the ending of my side of the story. So without further due here it is ……

Roxanne, Tom Dorgan and Co-author Mike McEniry
Transiting the Swinomish Channel in La Conner, WA

It was a sad day that I saw that view again, only it was with a new owner waving good-bye and his friend at the helm as it motored away out of my life. A sad day.

--next?

111

TWENTY-FOUR *ECHO SUMMIT* FOREVER

On one of our many visits to Victoria, Hal and I attended an exhibition of local artists. We ended up buying an oil painting... "Herring Run on the Gorge", artist Ernie Hertzog. We met Ernie and found he was a retired Royal Canadian Mountie. We liked the painting so much and liked his style, so suggested he might be interested in doing a painting of our boat. Hal contacted him, and the correspondence began.

"Dear Ernie:
 We are delighted you are willing to paint our boat! Time is no problem at all. The price is agreeable. Signed Henry." A snapshot was sent.

"Dear Henry (Hal) and Patsy,
I am pleased to be able to tell you that the painting of your boat is finished and in my view, has turned out quite nicely in the forest setting you were interested in. When next in Victoria give me a phone call and I will bring it to you at your boat."

We quickly cruised to Victoria in the *ECHO SUMMIT* and met Ernie and his family at the Oakbay Marina. When Hal welcomed them aboard, Ernie said, "I didn't think the boat was this big!"

The unveiling of the picture was quite a presentation. We were more than pleased. It was a special event with tea and cookies. Now we will always have the *ECHO SUMMIT* with us

Painting by Ernie Hertzog of *ECHO SUMMIT*

TWENTY-FIVE   PASSING THE TORCH

My son Scott continued the family passion for boating, essentially sailing. I asked him to say a few words for this book. The following pages are in his words.

Salt water. It covers four fifths of the earth. We begin our lives floating in it. We end our lives returning to it. It makes up most of what flows in our veins. It is integral to our being, and for some of us the desire, *the need,* to be near it, in it, on it, is inexorable. It may manifest right away, or become a dawning realization when a land-bound existence becomes untenable. Salt water. For me, it was a slow process that didn't come to fruition until my mid-twenties, but had roots that started much earlier.

When I was five, my dad decided to take up sailing. He took advantage of an offer from the Kool cigarette company for a 'Snark' sailing dinghy for $88 plus an 'end' from a carton of KOOLs. The boat was very similar to a 'Sunfish'; 11 ft. long, low freeboard, a 'lateen' rig, and was made entirely of Styrofoam. I have no memories of sailing in this boat with my dad, but it was destined to become my "first" boat. When I was 11, she became mine, and my journey to salt water began, albeit on fresh water. I learned much in that boat, plying the waters of Yarrow Bay on Lake Washington, eventually sailing into the lake proper, and one epic journey from the marina to the other side of the floating bridge off Evergreen Point.

My dad's second boat was destined to become my second boat as well. I was six when the Seattle Yacht Club was updating their dinghy fleet and put their existing fleet of 'Penguins' on the market. The Penguin was a 12-ft. open catboat with a Bermuda rig. I have several memories of sailing in this boat with my dad and sister on

Lake Washington. She seemed large at the time, but I was small and much of my world was large. I remember being awed by how large the waters we sailed on, and relatively tiny our boat was, particularly during a *near-capsize*. Was it a jibe, a gust, inattention on the helm? Dunno, but do remember the flood of water suddenly coming aboard as Dad, cursing and bellowing like an enraged bull, did his best to keep the boat upright amidst the cacophony of flogging sails and screaming children. When I was twelve she was bequeathed to me, in desperate need of refit. Fueled by dreams of freedom and adventure, I set to with a will, painting, repairing, varnishing, and saving money for a new aluminum mast, the wood one having succumbed to rot. Launching in the summer, I sailed the same waters covered by the snark, and with a larger boat was able to expand my range, covering the northern Lake Washington and even circumnavigating Mercer Island.

My dad's third boat was the gateway to what was to become the passion that has molded my life and continues to hold me in its briny grip. A Coronado 25 allowed him to slip the landlocked boundaries of the lake and ply the expanse of Puget sound. The Coronado 25 was a well-built modified fin keel boat with a spade rudder and an actual cabin. I was seven when my dad acquired her, and she was huge in comparison to the Penguin. The large waves and expanses of water found on Puget Sound were terrifying to a boy of seven who was used to the comparatively placid waters of Lake Washington, but over time there was joy to be found in taking the helm and sailing hard on the wind, spray flying as the boat bashed through waves as high as the rail. My dad, sister, and I explored the waters of Puget Sound venturing as far north as Port Ludlow and as far south as Gig Harbor. We learned how to cruise in the autumnal gales that lashed Puget Sound from the south, and bonded together in a time where the necessity for bonding was sorely needed. I would remember this boat well, as her sister ship plays a significant part in my story.

The fourth boat my father owned was an Islander 30, a fin keeled coastal sloop built for the demanding waters to be found off the coast of California. I was 11 when she came into our life. She was roomy, fast, and remarkably stiff in a breeze. This boat allowed us to explore Puget Sound from Gig Harbor to Port Townsend and thoroughly ensured that salt water had me in its grip.

Fast forward now to my 22nd year. I'd been living on the shores of Bellingham Bay, the San Juan Islands visible beyond Lummi Island that marked the western boundary of the Bay. Growing up cruising with my dad had never taken us as far north as the San Juan's, and the draw of the islands so close gnawed at my soul. Spurred on by my girlfriend I purchased my first real cruising boat, a Coronado 25! I was very familiar with the layout but it was now time to really learn what sailing was about. The waters of Bellingham Bay can be some of the nastiest found in the Salish Sea (the Salish Sea is a relatively new appellation for the inland waters of Washington State and encompass Puget Sound, the Straits of Juan de Fuca, and the various sounds, straits, bays and channels that surround the San Juan Islands.) Twenty miles of southern fetch combined with shoaling waters create a steep, short, nasty chop that requires constant vigilance and seamanship to master, particularly when sailing a boat with a balky outboard motor. The learning curve was as steep as the chop that was the blackboard for the lessons, but the boat was stout enough to make mistakes, learning opportunities rather than disasters. It's at this point that my bond with salt water was forged into the unbreakable bond holding me fast today..

When sailing with my dad, the Coronado had always been characterized as 'tender', due to her habit of rolling to the rail anytime the wind blew hard enough to ripple the water. As a new sailor this was very disconcerting and I became an expert at reefing down. One fine summer day found me sailing along the east side of Lummi Island, a formidable shoreline that plunged almost straight down from an 800-ft. height all the way down to the 100-ft.

116

depth of the sea bottom. In a southwesterly breeze, this had the effect of accelerating the wind that made it over the top of the island to create vicious and capricious gusts along the channel. One of them found me under full sail blissfully unaware of the danger. The gusts laid me right over. There was a metallic-sounding *PING* and I looked up to see the mast buckling at the spreaders before toppling ignominiously over the side. What followed were several hours of trying to secure the rig and limp back to the harbor. Insurance paid for a new mast, and I was back on the water in a matter of weeks.

The Coronado gave me the means to explore the islands and discover the majesty that they held. To this day, the scent that calms me beyond all others is salt and evergreens, an aroma that pervades many a quiet anchorage to be found in and amongst the islands. Cruising the islands ignited a wanderlust that could only be satisfied by getting a boat capable of tackling the oceans of the earth. I found a CT 34 gathering mold and barnacles in Tacoma and bought her for a song with my fiancé. The CT 34 is a double-ended, full keel cutter designed from the start with ocean cruising in mind. We spent two years refitting her before finally launching in the spring of 1991.

I was excited to experience sailing in a full keel boat, as the tenderness of the Coronado was still freshly imprinted in my mind. Imagine my consternation during my first sail when she rolled right to the rail as soon as the wind got up to ten knots! I had thought that a full keel would impart a much stiffer ride but through trial and error I realized that, while she would roll right over, she would always stick at the rail. While heavy gusts or strong winds might bury the rail in green water, it was after the roll that the incredible stability of a full keel design became apparent. Not only was she rock solid at that point, but she tracked in a straight line even when the helm was unmanned. In retrospect, I realized that the Coronado had offered the same stability, if not the tracking, that the full keel design imparted. I became a dedicated member of the 'full keel fan club', and never looked back.

Divorce has a way of scuppering even the best laid plans, and mine left me without a boat at all. This was a mixed blessing, as the CT had a host of issues that I was happy to leave in 'my Ex's hands'. On the other side of the coin was the incredibly poor straits I now found myself. I managed to scrimp and save some money, but not enough to buy the type of boat I actually wanted. Still nursing the dream of going cruising on blue water, I decided to pursue a wood boat, as I could get a tremendous bang for my buck. So, it was in the spring of 1993 that "*IANTHE*" came into my life, and started the love affair with wood boats that plagues me still.

IANTHE was a 1939 Rodd English Channel sloop, a one design patterned after the Channel pilot boats of England. She featured a plumb bow, a full keel, with a graceful overhang that terminated in a tiny transom. She sported a fractional Marconi sloop rig, and very quickly became an extension of my being. She lived for 15+ knots of wind, and would happily beat to weather all day with a bone in her teeth. It was off the wind, however, where she really came into her own, fairly leaping off the swells that rolled in from Anacortes on those single tack fifteen-mile legs from Cypress Island that seemed to fill my autumn days. I was working to pay her off and head south to sun-drenched beaches of Mexico when I met the woman who would give me my son Liam. She was game to go cruising, but the arrival of our only child three years later sunk the dream again. I sold *IANTHE* in 1998 and boating took a back seat to raising my boy.

I enjoyed my second divorce in 2005 and *IANTHE* came back into my life when I partnered with the man who'd bought her from me seven years prior. I was able to instill the love of sailing in my son who was as yet unaware of the hold salt water would have on his soul. Together we explored the San Juan's, and the childlike wonder he brought to the adventure resonates with me still.

Exploring the shallow caves of Sucia Island, learning to row and sail a dinghy, learning how to helm a boat on a course that would cover the shortest distance between two points. It was these moments and more, created a bond between us, the same bond shared with my own father, the experience of wind and water and no need for words.

In 2009, a dear friend bequeathed me with a 1946 40-ft. Owens, a full keel cutter that became the basis for the wildly successful Hinckley Bermuda Ketch. She was the precursor to 'cold molding', with a double-sheathed plywood hull covered in carvel planks. This created a very strong, very light hull that was a dream to sail. The added waterline makes seven knots the standard cruising speed under sail, and allowed for many a trip to the far reaches of the San Juan's. While a joy to sail, this boat never got under my skin. Of all my boats, she's the only one I couldn't love. Forty feet of wood boat proved to be far too much for one person to keep up, and unable to find a partner, I finally sold her in 2016. I now had the pleasure of looking for a boat unbound by price (to a certain degree) or compromise (typically required when a woman is part of the decision-making process of any sort.) One thing was certain, however, the next boat would be fiberglass as I was weary of the work required of a wood boat.

I suppose, had I been listening, the sound of the universe laughing at me would have been audible. Fate is fickle, and wood boats were almost as much a part of me as salt water. I looked at several glass boats and always found reason to reject them; *too sterile, too thin, slappy water on the hull, or too high of freeboard.* Ultimately it came down to a single common denominator: *Fiberglass boats have incomplete souls.* The lines can be pleasing to the eye, a well-crafted wooden interior could almost fool one into thinking there were vestiges of life within, but they always lacked the vital spark that comes from a vessel crafted from material that once was alive. A wood boat moving through salt water is a song sung through the years, creating a joy felt by mariners for millennia, an almost silent hiss of seething foam and spray. The tug of wood was strong, and when **'TULLAMORE'** came on the market, I knew I was lost.

Everything about her was wrong.... She was wood for one thing. She had no 'standing head room'. Her interior was more suited to day-sailing than cruising. She was gaff-rigged, which meant windward performance would be wretched. The engine was old and tired and sure to need replacement. Varnish and paint were peeling, and she hadn't been hauled in several years. "I'll just drive down to Anacortes for a look," I told myself. "I'm not about to buy another wood boat, but she's so damn salty, it'd be a shame not to at least take a peek". Three hours later the offer was made, accepted, and I was the owner of the best boat of my life. It was love at first sight.

TULLAMORE is an Atkins Gary Thomas design in 1949. She's 26-ft. on deck, 30-ft. overall, a full keel gaff rigged topsail cutter built in 1997 at the NW School for Wooden Boat Building, and is a beautiful to look at as she is to sail. The gaff rig was the traditional choice for working sail through the nineteenth century and early part of the 20th century as it delivers a tremendous amount of sail area that is relatively easy to handle, performs well on all points of sail, and is very, very fast. I say performs well on all points of sail, and at the turn of the last century when the rig was in its heyday this was true. The modern 'Bermuda' rig, brought on by sailing becoming mainstream, is comparatively easier to handle and imparts incredible ability to point into the wind, thirty degrees being a comfortable norm. Full keel versions, as I discovered, suffered from the long keel and were typically only capable of pointing thirty-five to forty degrees to the wind. A full keeled gaff cutter, on the other hand, is lucky to see forty-five. She makes up for it on anything below a close reach and flies through the water as if the devil were at her heels. The 'first reef' is to hand the tops'l, and this typically occurs around 12 to 15 knots of wind. She's good up to 20, and then the first reef in the main is taken. This is good up to

30, and then the second reef should be next. This is conjecture on my part, as the last time I was in 30 knots of wind I decided to call it a day and head in. I'm not sure at what level the next sail reduction would occur, but suspect around 35, when I bring in the jib... an unpleasant prospect to consider as it would happen at the end of a wildly pitching bowsprit. I think she'd be good in up to 50 knots under 2nd reefed main and stays'l, but I hope to find out by chance rather than design.

TULLAMORE is in the middle of a two-year refit which is primarily cosmetic in nature, renewing paint and varnish. There are some larger projects yet to do as well. The old engine has reached the point of diminishing returns on investment and a repower is currently in the works. She needs heat, and a combination diesel stove/heater will maximize the very limited space afforded in a pocket cruiser of this size. Her electrical system needs updating and with the very capable hands of my son Liam to help, she will be in great shape for new adventures come spring. Liam earns the right to sail her when I am not by helping maintain and refit, and has already experienced adventures in her that need telling. They are his tales to tell, however, and I will leave it to him to write his own story.

Fair winds and following seas.......

S.V. TULLAMORE

My Grand-son, Liam McEniry acquired his 'first' boat at age eleven. It was found in a farmer's field, resting on a trailer, out in Whatcom County. It had been in that field for some time and one could readily see that it was a "project boat". Some research determined the model. It was a "Glen L-17".

Three years of hard work later it was christened **FALCON** and launched into Bellingham Bay, under the guarded eye of his father, Scott. –it didn't sink.

Liam's first boat, FALCON, a Glen L-17

As of this writing, Liam has decided to forego college in favor of earning a Marine Electrician's commercial rating. (It is a very specialized field and, with the rating, is a sure guard against the fluctuations of a variable economy. He intends on 'living on a boat'. (I wonder how long that will hold up when a Lady enters his life to stay. There isn't much closet space on a sailboat.)

Stay tuned for Part Two, **The Bamfield Odyssey.**

PART TWO

THE BAMFIELD ODYSSEY

By Patsy Love

May 1958

It started with a phone call. My husband, Hal, told me of a twenty-six-foot missing charter boat that had been found beached on Vancouver Island. He went on to say, "Do you want to go with Paul and me to bring it back? If so, I'll call mother to see if she will take care of the girls."

I was delighted to go on a short boat trip, a little get-away from the care of two small children and household chores. It didn't take me long to pack my bag. Hal neglected to tell me the boat was ditched on the OCEAN side of Vancouver Island B.C.'s rugged coast... clear up in Barkley Sound at a little hamlet called Bamfield.

When this bizarre story of the stolen boat hit the papers, Hal recognized the Boat Charter Service as the one he used when fishing with out of town friends. He called them and offered to bring the boat back to Seattle. He then, was referred to the insurance company, and an okay was arranged. "Save your receipts."

Hal and I, along with Paul Speyer, one of Hal's fishing buddies, flew on a commercial flight to Vancouver, B.C. the following Friday morning. We did a little shopping and had a nice lunch at the Hotel Vancouver. Hal made arrangements to charter a plane across the island to Banfield. At the Charter Service Hal asked for a chart of the area and was given an old "Aeronautical edition". The chart did not cover all of the Straits of Juan de Fuca to Port Angeles. To get to our destination, Hal needed a better chart, a nautical chart.

Coast Guard Seeking Child, 12, Stepfather

A Seattle man and his 12½-year-old stepdaughter, missing since Saturday when they went cruising on Puget Sound in a 26-foot boat, were the object of a Coast Guard air and sea search Monday.

The two, Darrell A. Rubens, 34, and Linda Irene Rubens, 2108 10th Ave. N., were reported missing Sunday afternoon by Mrs. Helen Rubens, 28, wife and mother.

The Coast Guard said the boat, rented from ABC Charters in Seattle, was last seen passing through Hiram Chittenden Locks at 3:25 p. m. Saturday.

MRS. HELEN RUBENS, who was at work in a University District photographic studio when her husband and daughter left home, said he didn't tell her they were going on a boat trip. Her first information of it was when she learned a book on navigation Rubens had been reading was missing.

"The whole family just likes the water," Mrs. Rubens explained.

"My husband, especially, is crazy about the water, although he doesn't know anything about navigation. We have been going down to Lake Union, looking at the boats, and dreaming about the day when we could own a boat of our own."

MRS. RUBENS said her husband has talked frequently about "all the uninhabited islands and how he would like to explore one." She thought it likely that they could have become lost, either on the water or on some remote island.

"There has been quite a bit of adventure thought of and talked about in our family," she said. "Lately, the three of us have been

(Continued Page 10, Column 3)

Coast Guard Seeking Pair

(Continued from Page 1.)

talking of going to Florida and living on an island of our own. It's a dream we all have shared."

The Rubens family came here from Helena, Mont., a year ago. Rubens works for a grocery chain and occasionally plays with local orchestras. His instruments are the saxophone and clarinet.

Linda Irene, a talented pianist, is in the seventh grade at Meany Junior High School.

HER MOTHER SAID that Linda Irene is a "striking child, large enough to pass for 15."

The girl was wearing her blonde hair in a long pony-tail, the mother said. She is five feet one inch tall and weighs 105 pounds. She was wearing a black car coat with a white collar, pedal pushers and black suede shoes.

Rubens was wearing faded jeans with a patch on the right hip pocket, a charcoal brown sport shirt and a brown jacket with gray stripes, his wife reported.

He has blue eyes and brown hair, is six feet tall and weighs 175 pounds. Part of his right heel and kneecap were shot away while he was serving with the Army in World War II, his wife said.

Hal met with the pilot to discuss the flight plan. The pilot's accent told us he was "French Canadian". These 'bush pilots' were held in high regard for their ability to fly in and out of remote wilderness areas.

Hal, Paul and I climbed aboard the De Havilland Beaver float plane in the afternoon with our baggage and my small 'Brownie' box camera. We flew from Vancouver, B.C. across the island and up to Barkley Sound.

Dressed for the 'big city', not the 'wilderness'.

"Where do you want me to land?" the pilot asked.

I looked out the window from my seat in this small plane and saw nothing but trees and ocean. Hal pointed to the little hamlet of Bamfield. The pilot made a smooth landing and taxied up to a dock. There were no roads into Bamfield at that time.

We were met by a couple of mechanics in their skiff, ready to take Hal and Paul down the channel to the Marine Repair. I remained on the dock with my suitcase, dressed in clothes suitable for shopping in Vancouver.... a linen suit

127

with black velvet collar and *high heels!* My boat clothes were in my suitcase. Where to go to make the change? I looked around.

There was a small store near the dock and two houses up on the hill. Across the channel, a building identified as the 'Cable Station'. Soon, a woman walked down to the dock and asked if I needed help. I told her my predicament which she solved by inviting me to her home. Her husband was the 'LIFEBOAT' tender who had brought the missing boat into Bamfield. It had been beached on the west shore of Vancouver Island.

I put on my boat clothes, thanked her, and walked back to the dock. Hal and Paul were not there yet. While still waiting for the fellas to bring the boat, two old fishermen came to my rescue and invited me aboard their fishing schooner for a cup of tea. I remember looking at one fisherman's gnarled hands while he talked about the wild flowers of the area. Those hands were full of fish hook scars and calluses from hard work.

Finally, the little twenty-six-foot power boat came cruising slowly down the channel from the Marine Repair. with Hal at the helm. The repairs were not perfect, but Hal was told the boat *SHOULD* be in good enough shape to get us to Seattle safely. The shaft was still a bit bent and the prop was really bent. Both conditions will affect the engine RPM's, resulting in less power.

Paul and I went aboard and started to clean out the bedding, etc. Soon a few Indians showed up to take all unwanted items. Hal was busy filling the two gas tanks that the cruiser was equipped with. He paid with his personal 'Shell' credit card. But, as luck would have it, the card slipped out of his fingers and dropped between the boards into the water. (I don't remember how that problem was solved.)

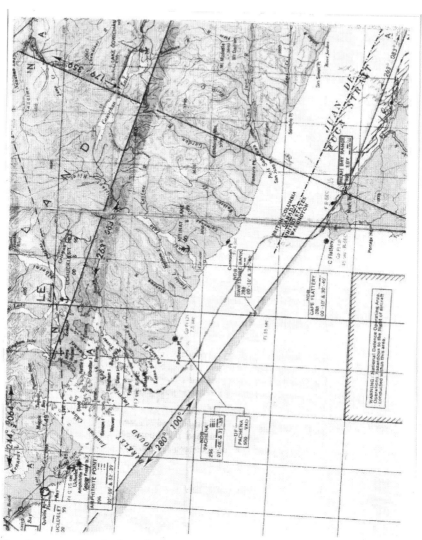

An _Aeronautical_ chart is meant for aircraft, barely usable for a boat. This was before GPS, of course.

Later, the Customs/Postmaster invited us to come to his home and pick up the box of liquor confiscated from the boat. The box included a bottle of 'Mogen David' sweet

129

wine. It was social invitation too, with libation and conversation.

Patsy and the 26 ft. cruiser

The customs officer explained that the LIFEBOAT tender (a branch of the Canadian Coast Guard) found the missing boat and the missing persons, a man and a twelve-year old girl, walking along the rugged coastline. They looked wet and bedraggled and hadn't eaten for two days. The man was missing a shoe.

The LIFEBOAT tender towed the little cruiser, with the survivors, into Bamfield and the United States Coast Guard was alerted. Royal Canadian Mounties then took them to Victoria and put them aboard a plane to Seattle.

Back at the dock, while cleaning out the boat, we found a World Map and a sack of dried beans, among other things. There were no life jackets, no Radar or radio, or survival equipment—just some 'flotation cushions', hardly suitable for launching into the Pacific Ocean and a slow trip south to the Strait of Juan de Fuca before reaching the sheltered waters of Puget Sound.

The couple was found by The Bamfield Lifeboat at Canadian Coast Guard Station, Bamfield, B.C. It was a 'search-and-rescue' vessel, wooden hulled, diesel powered surf boat, able to right herself in heavy seas. It is now on display in Port Alberni.

End Of Excursion

DARRELL A. RUBENS, 34, and his stepdaughter, Linda Irene, 12, step from plane at the Seattle-Tacoma International Airport yesterday after being missing since Saturday. The two were found on the west side of Vancouver Island after they hiked some nine miles through a wilderness in search of fuel for their cabin cruiser. —(Post-Intelligencer photo by John M. "Heck" Miller)

Boating Pair Back; Police Arrest Man

At 5:30 the next morning we left Bamfield in the twenty-six-foot, now underpowered due to shaft and prop damage, and headed out into the Pacific Ocean. We were following the fishing fleet and screeching seagulls. The skies were overcast.

The deep ocean swells hid the fishing boat ahead of us at times. There was a huge wall of water in between. Of the three of us, Hal was the only one who could handle the small cruiser in those big ocean swells. He had to keep the boat from turning sideways in the deep troughs.... which could cause the boat to capsize. We learned later that they were sometimes described as *"Roller-Coaster North Pacific swells"*.

I had planned on fixing breakfast while underway, but that was out of the question. The atmosphere aboard was full of tension and anxiety.... Not much conversation. We just worked on keeping our balance as Hal conquered each ocean swell.

The under-powered cruised slowly past the Swift Shure Lightship (marking the International Boundary) just before 10:30 AM.

It had taken five hours to reach US waters.

WE MADE IT. Neah Bay... familiar waters at last. Hal had been at the helm for five hours, fighting heaving ocean waves, and the broaching or swamping.

We were grateful the little boat, with a bent shaft and scrambled prop, still had enough power to make the crossing. The rest of the way to Seattle and Lake Union should be easy. The little cruiser had made it through the heavy ocean swells without a mishap. On with our journey.

After lunch we continued down the 'Straits' to Sekiu and tied up for the night. The three of us ate a real dinner at a restaurant near the dock. What a story the fellas had to tell at the bar later!

A Happy Crew having made it to Neah Bay

The next morning Hal and Paul took time enough for the early morning 'fish bite'. Good luck was with them...two fish were in the boat. By 11:00 AM we were on our way down the 'Straits' toward Port Angeles.

Always time for some fishing

"We can stay there overnight and finish our trip to Seattle on Monday", Hal suggested. Paul and I agreed it was a good plan.

This was Sunday, "Mother's Day", a beautiful sunny, breezy day. We were enjoying this 'rescue' trip. An hour later we noticed the breeze getting a little stronger. The wind was kicking up a bit. Hal could not check the Weather Channel for gale warnings.... no radio.

I looked at the Aeronautical Chart for thoughts of finding a little cove where we could get in out of the stormy weather. The chart ended a few miles past Sekiu. Now no chart to guide us.

The wind was soon blowing into a gale. This was a real storm with white caps on the waves. The bow of the boat rose sharply at the crest of each wave. Then, with sickening speed, down into the troughs, waiting for the next wave, just as big. With the reduced power, the boat was struggling.

Hal had real concerns about staying upright and afloat, finally turning into a small bay off Crescent Beach, hoping to get out of the rough water. The shallow bay made big waves... so big they were splashing over the cabin. Panic set in.

"Let's beach the boat", Paul yelled out over the sound of wind and waves.

Hal answered, "The boat will be smashed to pieces, and us too, by the force of the waves."

He told Paul to find some flares. "We need help!" he added.

Paul found a flare and set it off while Hal steered the boat making wide circles.

We found out later that a picnicking family saw the flare, and noticed our boat in distress. The man of the family ran to the phone in the park and called the Coast Guard station in Port Angeles. (This was before cell phones.)

134

In due time a Coast Guard helicopter responded. The only way the pilot could communicate with us was by sending down messages on a line to the deck of our boat. The messages were written and enclosed in a block of wood, satin ribbon attached.

MESSAGES: *ARE YOU IN DISTRESS? IF YOU ARE IN DISTRESS, HOLD ARMS STRAIGHT UP.*
IF YOU NEED A TOW, HOLD ARMS STRAIGHT OUT
IF YOU LOST SOMEONE OVERBOARDD, LAY DOWN

Hal wrote back, "*WE HAVE VERY LITTLE POWER, SHALL WE BEACH THE BOAT?*" He stuffed his answer in the wood block and attached it to the line.

Paul and I held our arms straight up—for 'Distress', then we held our arms straight out— 'For a Tow'.

The pilot pulled the line up and put another message in the block. *83-FOOTER IS ON THE WAY. BE HERE IN 1 HR.* Then he landed the helicopter on the beach where we could see it. This action gave us moral support.

Meanwhile, Hal had another problem. He was going to have to switch from one fuel tank to another without the engine losing power. He and Paul talked about it and Paul pushed the button to switch. It worked, the boat continued running.

So, Hal had to fight the waves and stay afloat for one more hour. He had no respite from the helm.

It was a joyful sight to see the 83-foot Coast Guard

135

cutter ploughing through the stormy seas to rescue us—so stormy, in fact, one seaman was seasick enroute.

If we had had a *nautical* chart of the area, we could have checked it for a deeper cove giving our boat more cover. (--mark that up as a serious blunder from the beginning.)

The Coast Guard cutter made a 'trough' for Hal to navigate to a protected cove, sheltered from the storm. I was taken off the little cruiser and transferred to the Coast Guard cutter for the rest of the journey. I couldn't stop shaking. I was in shock.

Hal steered the little cruiser in the trough of the Coast guard cutter all the way to Port Angeles. Three seamen stood at the stern, guarding. More than once, the waves caused Hal to nearly plough into the back of the ship. The slow trip seemed to take forever.

We arrived in Port Angeles late in the evening feeling most beholden to our life savers. What could we do to show our appreciation for coming to our rescue? Someone told us, "After a rescue, the seamen head for a certain tavern."

After safely tied to the dock, we walked to that tavern and found the crew. Hal and Paul gave them several rounds of libation for a BIG THANK YOU! We were more than grateful to them for saving our lives.

The next morning Hal, Paul and I took the ferry back to Seattle.

The following weekend, Hal and Dave (another fishing buddy) came up to Port Angeles and brought the damaged twenty-six-footer back to Lake Union. Paul and I declined. I was very glad to stay home and be a mother.

Respect for my husband rose 200%. He had remained 'cool' and did what needed to be done while others panicked on this boat trip.

-END-

EPILOGUE

Hal and I revisited the remote hamlet of Bamfield, on the western side of Vancouver Island, in the 1980's.

It was a beautiful drive up the east coast of the island to Port Alberni. Starting from Victoria, we drove through Ladysmith, and on to Nanaimo. The highway continues through old growth firs in a park-like setting. A few miles ahead we stopped to take in the view of the Straits of Georgia—then on to Parksville and Port Alberni.

The next morning, we boarded the 'freight boat', "Lady Rose" with six other passengers—off for a day trip down the Alberni Canal. The Captain welcomed us aboard.

"Coffee's on below. Make yourself at home." --a casual atmosphere. He then went back to the supervision of loading the freight and supplies for the little hamlets along the way.

The Engineer, besides loading and unloading cargo and checking the engine, worked the galley grill. No menu, "I can fix bacon & eggs, if you're hungry."

When all the supplies were loaded, we cast off, heading down the Canal to Bamfield.

Seeing Bamfield again was true nostalgia. It had been at least twenty-five years since we set out toward the ocean, from Bamfield to Neah Bay in a 26-foot under-powered cruiser.

The dock was the same. The store was the same, with more merchandise. We bought ice-cream cones. Hal took pictures with a better camera.

--not quite The End....

137

BACK AGAIN

In 2012, after Hal died, I talked Robin, and her husband Richard, into making the same trip to Port Alberni and beyond. I saw many changes.

The ship "Lady Rose" had been retired after fifty years of service and replaced with the 128-foot "Francis Barkley". On the sunny September day that we took the day trip, there were seventy-five passengers. The Ship's Galley Coffee Shop had a menu now with moderate prices.

We watched the loading of supplies and freight and saw the same stops along the way, lumber camps—Kildonan and others. The three-day schedule was the same; leaving building supplies, fuel, equipment, groceries, and mail—then picking up garbage, mail, etc., to go. People live different lives along the Canal.

CHANGES IN BAMFIELD – There was a new sign on the dock. The Cable Station, perched on the other side of the inlet, that was the terminus of the first transpacific telegraph cable is now a combined marine coastal science laboratory and classroom complex. The little Customs House on the hill where we picked up the confiscated liquor many years ago was gone. A rough gravel logging road now leads into Bamfield.

The store was still in the same place on the side of the hill. It closed while the owner was getting supplies from the boat. We walked along the narrow path past a few rustic cottages and came upon a 'cat' village. There were quaint little 'cat' houses that gave shelter to the feral cats in the area. A sign said, "Please donate to feed the cats." We did.

The store opened in time to get ice cream cones before leaving.

The route back to Port Alberni gave us the opportunity to see wild life, including eagles and whales.

138

One whale broached the surface of the water and showed its tail in the late afternoon sun.

I have become fascinated with the rugged west coast life on Vancouver Island, with the history and the people who lived there. Our exciting, fearful experience that started in Bamfield will always stay in my memory.

Bamfield, Canada & the 'Cat House'

128 ft. "Francis Barkley"

Richard & Patsy   *Robin & Patsy*

The End

78071578R00080

Made in the USA
San Bernardino, CA
02 June 2018